Fundamentals of Western Music

Also from Wadsworth . . .

Basic Musicianship: An Introduction to Music Fundamentals with Computer Assistance
Raynold Allvin

Foundations in Music Theory: With Programmed Exercises, Second Edition
Leon Dallin

Theoretical Foundations of Music
William Duckworth and Edward Brown

Basic Musicianship for Classroom Teachers: A Creative Musical Approach
Charles R. Hoffer and Marjorie Hoffer

Basic Concepts in Music, Second Edition
Gary Martin

Harmony and Melody, Volumes 1 and 2
Elie Siegmeister

Workbooks for Harmony and Melody, Volumes 1 and 2
Elie Siegmeister

Introduction to Music Reading, Concepts and Applications, Second Edition
William Thomson

Functional Harmony, Volumes 1 and 2
William Toutant

Fundamentals of Western Music

Marion and Neil McKay
University of Hawaii at Manoa

Wadsworth Publishing Company
Belmont, California
A Division of Wadsworth, Inc.

Music Editor: Sheryl Fullerton
Production Editor: Deborah O. McDaniel
Managing Designer: Merle Sanderson
Print Buyer: Barbara Britton
Designer: Diane Hillier
Copy Editor: David Hathwell
Music Engraver: Ernie Mansfield
Cover: Merle Sanderson
Signing Representative: Lorenda Pezzola Phillips

Printed in the United States of America
    8 9 10—97 96 95

ISBN 0-534-05106-5

Library of Congress Cataloging in Publication Data

McKay, Marion.
Fundamentals of Western music.

Includes index.
1. Music—Theory, Elementary.
I. McKay, Neil.   II.   Title.
MT7.M4215   1986   781   85-6332
ISBN 0-534-05106-5

To Nancy and Ian

Contents

Preface

Music of the world is as diverse as the cultures that create it. Methods for transmitting musical ideas are equally varied. In Western civilization a system of notation has evolved that allows transmission of musical thought with utmost precision. The notation applies equally to all genres, whether symphony, folk music, popular music, or jazz.

This book is an introduction to reading and notating Western music. It is designed to serve as a textbook for a one-semester course at the college level. Students need no prior knowledge of music. The course of study will foster an understanding of and appreciation for the roles of composer, performer, and listener.

Beginning with a discussion of a musical tone and its characteristics, the text then discusses the notation of durations in metric and rhythmic groupings, the notation of pitch and its organization in scales, keys, and intervals, and finally combinations of duration and pitch culminating in melody and harmony. Later chapters deal with more advanced rhythmic and pitch organization and present an introduction to the forms of music. The book is arranged so that, as much as possible, chapters concerning pitch alternate with chapters dealing with duration. In the authors' experience, such alternation is essential in maintaining student interest and is more conducive to assimilation and retention. However, instructors who wish to present chapters in a different order will find that the book has the flexibility to accommodate them.

The book's course of study provides skills that enable students to read and sing music of folk-song difficulty. Exercises for each chapter test the student's progress. Musical examples with words, which makes music seem less abstract, culminate in the student's writing a melody and accompaniment for a short poem. For instructors who wish to use the piano as a laboratory instrument, piano exercises based on the material of each chapter are included.

The authors wish to acknowledge the assistance of colleagues at the University of Hawaii—Don Conover, Gary Danchenka, Dorothy Gillett, Marvin Greenberg, Marian Guck, Irene Levenson, Armand Russell, Allen Trubitt, Floyd Uchima, Byron Yasui—who, with helpful suggestions and encouragement, used this book as a text in its formative stages.

They also wish to thank the reviewers—Phillip Browne, California State Polytechnic College; Anthony Ginter, University of California, Riverside; Jeanne Knorr, Towson State University; and Fred Weber, American River College—whose thoughtful criticism and comments were useful and appreciated.

1

Musical Sound: Its Origin and Characteristics

TONE

Music is a series of tones experienced within a period of time. The representation of these tones on paper and how this musical **notation** is read and interpreted are fundamental to the study of Western music.

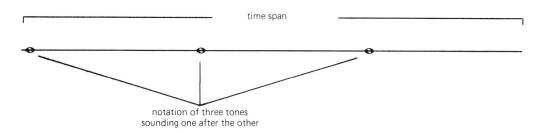

time span

notation of three tones
sounding one after the other

The term *tone* is to be distinguished from the term *sound*, as sound encompasses all aural impressions. Random sound is noise and is the result of irregular vibrations of a vibrating body. Tone is a refinement of sound as the result of regular vibrations.

sound ⟨ tone (regular vibrations)
noise (irregular vibrations)

Tone is initiated by a vibrating body. For instruments such as those of the violin family the vibrating body is a string that is plucked or bowed. A piano string is struck by a hammer. The vibrating body of drums is a taut membrane, also struck, and for wind instruments it is a column of air within the hollow tube of the instrument itself. However the vibration is initiated, it causes waves to be set up in the air that eventually strike the eardrum as sound.

To understand musical sound a single tone must be examined. A single tone has four characteristics: **pitch**, **intensity**, **duration**, and **timbre**.

PITCH

Pitch is the location of the tone in a high-low sound spectrum. A high tone is the result of rapid vibration of the vibrating body. Conversely, slow vibration produces a low pitch. Pitch also depends upon the length and thickness of the vibrating body. A brief examination of the piano or harp reveals that the long, thick strings produce low pitches, whereas the short, thin strings produce high pitches. Larger wind instruments produce lower sounds than smaller ones because the air columns are longer and thicker. Pitch is also affected by air pressure. For example, because air pressure constantly fluctuates, string and wind instruments must constantly be adjusted to remain "in tune."

1.1 Ear Exercises: Pitch

Instructor:

1. *Matching pitches.* Play a pitch and its octave on the piano. Have students sing the pitch on a neutral syllable (such as *ah, la,* or *loo*).

   Example:

   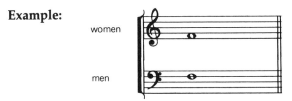

   Repeat with other pitches.

2. *Differentiating higher and lower pitches.* Play consecutively two different pitches in octaves. Have students match the pitches and note whether the second pitch is higher or lower than the first.

Examples:

Repeat with other consecutive pitches.

1.2 Reading Exercises: Pitch

With two tones represented in space as lower, ʊ, and higher, ᴑ, sing the following on a neutral syllable.[1]

1.

Instructor: Give first two pitches. Exercise 1 should sound as follows:

Indicate each tone with a hand signal. Repeat with other tones.

2. duet
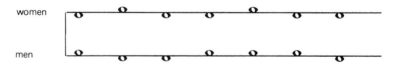

---

1. *In this and following chapters use neutral syllables unless otherwise indicated.*

Instructor: Give first two pitches. Exercise 2 should sound as follows:

INTENSITY

Intensity or loudness is caused by the amplitude of the vibrating body. Force causes wide vibration. If vibrations are created with great force the resulting tone will be loud, and if vibrations are created with little force the tone will be soft.

Intensity is represented in notation by symbols that are abbreviations of Italian words.

- *ff fortissimo*   very loud
- *f forte*   loud
- *mf mezzo forte*   moderately loud
- *mp mezzo piano*   moderately soft
- *p piano*   soft
- *pp pianissimo*   very soft

A gradual increase in intensity (***crescendo***, or *cresc.*) is indicated by diverging lines.

pp ——————————————————————— *ff*

A gradual decrease in intensity (***decrescendo***, or *decresc.*; alternatively ***diminuendo***, or *dim.*) is indicated by converging lines.

f ——————————————————————— *mp*

The terms signifying varying degrees of intensity are all relative. One performer's *piano* may be softer than another performer's, but however soft it is the *pianissimo* of each will be even softer.

All terms and symbols referring to intensity are called **dynamic markings** or simply **dynamics**.

1.3 Reading Exercises: Pitch and Intensity

Sing the following.

Instructor: Give pitches and hand signals as in Exercises 1.2.

1.

2. duet[2]

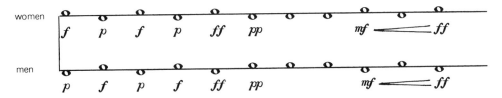

DURATION

Duration refers to how long a tone continues. Duration is limited by the instrument—for example, by the length of time a piano string vibrates or by the length of the bow of a string instrument. It is also limited by the performer—for example, by the breathing time of a singer or wind player. In notation, duration is mathematically measured, as one written tone has a duration directly proportionate to that of another.

---

2. *Where no dynamic marking is present, the intensity level remains the same as last indicated.*

1.4 Ear Exercises: Pitch, Intensity, and Duration

1. Sing short tones and long tones.

2. Listen to two tones of the same or differing pitch and differentiate as to which is shorter and longer.

1.5 Reading Exercises: Pitch, Intensity, and Duration

Sing the following. • = short tone (one second), ○ = long tone (four seconds).
Instructor: Seconds may be indicated in different ways—with metronome, tapping, or hand signals.

1.

2. duet

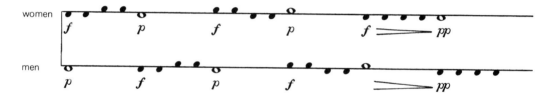

<table>
<tr><td>TIMBRE</td><td>

Timbre is tone quality. When a string vibrates it produces a fundamental tone that is the result of the vibration of the entire length of the string. At the same time it vibrates in sections with varying vibrating ratios. Simultaneous sympathetic vibrations are called **harmonics** or **partials** (discussed further in Chapter 7), and these give instruments their characteristic sounds. Timbre is a topic of great importance because a piece of music is written with a particular voice, instrument, or group of instruments in mind. Knowledge of the tone quality of an instrument is a necessity when writing for it alone or in combination with other instruments.

</td></tr>
</table>

TIMBRE

Timbre is tone quality. When a string vibrates it produces a fundamental tone that is the result of the vibration of the entire length of the string. At the same time it vibrates in sections with varying vibrating ratios. Simultaneous sympathetic vibrations are called **harmonics** or **partials** (discussed further in Chapter 7), and these give instruments their characteristic sounds. Timbre is a topic of great importance because a piece of music is written with a particular voice, instrument, or group of instruments in mind. Knowledge of the tone quality of an instrument is a necessity when writing for it alone or in combination with other instruments.

1. Each voice performing the previous exercises had its own tone quality. Perform the exercises again with different combinations of voices, noting the contrasts in timbre.

CHAPTER EXERCISES

1. Be able to match pitches, distinguish high and low pitches, and distinguish differences in intensity and duration.

2. Using the solid line below, notate your own series of tones incorporating high and low pitches, long and short durations, and indications for intensity as in the above exercises. Be able to perform it. Your voice will provide the timbre.

time span = twenty-four seconds

Example:

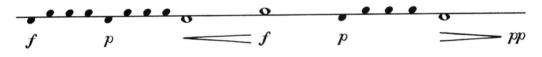

PIANO EXERCISES

Use any two pitches of the piano keyboard for the following exercises.

1. Play Exercise 1.2.1.

2. Play Exercise 1.3.1.

3. Play Exercise 1.5.1.

4. With another person play Exercise 1.5.2.

2

Duration

NOTES

The written symbols for sound in music are **notes**. Parts of a note are identified as follows.

— flag
— stem
— head

The note with the longest duration is the whole note, and the other notes represent fractions of the whole note.

- *whole note*   o

- *half note*

- *quarter note*

- *eighth note*

- *sixteenth note*

- *thirty-second note*

Note heads are oval in shape. They are open (white) for whole and half notes and solid (black) for notes of shorter duration. Stems are attached to the note head and extend up on the right, ♩, or down on the left, ♩. Flags are attached to the stem, one flag for eighth notes, ♪, two for sixteenth notes, ♬, and so on. Whether or not the stem is up or down, the flag is always to the right.

None of the above notes has an exact duration; rather, each has a relative duration of exactly half that of the previous note.

The following chart shows durational equivalents of the whole note.

- *one whole note equals*
- *two half notes equal*
- *four quarter notes equal*
- *eight eighth notes or[1] equal*
- *sixteen sixteenth notes or*

2.1 Reading Exercises: Duration

Each following exercise is twelve seconds in duration. If the whole note has a duration of four seconds, the half note will have a duration of two seconds and the quarter note a duration of one second. Two eighth notes will have a duration of one second, as will four sixteenth notes.

---

1. *To facilitate reading, **beams** are used for groups of notes that individually would require flags. The number of beams corresponds to the number of flags on a single note.*

1. Match a given pitch and sing the following, to the syllable *dah*. Observe the dynamic markings.

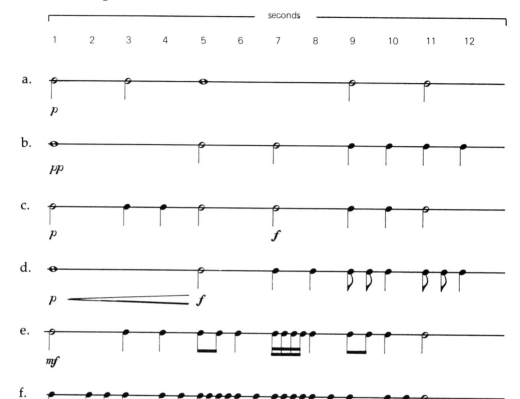

2. Match two given pitches[2] and sing the following.

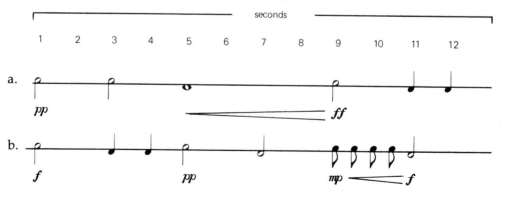

---

2. *Suggestion for instructor: a minor third.*

3. Duets. Proceed as in Exercise 2.

2.2 Writing Exercises: Duration

Write notes in the exercises below, spacing them according to the twelve-second chart. Durational relationships will correspond to those of the preceding reading exercises. (These exercises may be used for additional practice in reading.)

Example:

Write *below* the line with stems *up* the following succession of notes: four quarters, two eighths (beamed), four sixteenths (beamed), one half, one whole.

1. Write *on* the line (for example, ●) with stems *down* the following succession of notes: two half notes, three quarters, two eighths (with flags), one whole.

seconds

1 2 3 4 5 6 7 8 9 10 11 12

2. Write *above* the line with stems *down* the following succession of notes: one whole, one half, two quarters, four sixteenths (beamed), two eighths (beamed), one half.

3. Write *below* the line with stems *up* the following succession of notes: four eighths (beamed), one half, four quarters, one whole.

4. Invent and be able to perform a twelve-second succession of notes of varying durations, writing above and below the line to indicate high and low, and adding dynamics.

TIES

Durational values may be increased by the use of a **tie**, a curved line connecting notes of the same pitch, drawn at the head ends of the notes. In performance the tied notes sound as one tone, sustained for the total value of all of the tied notes.[3]

DOTS

A **dot**, written beside and to the right of a note head, increases the time value or duration of the note by one-half.[4] Some durational equivalents of dotted notes are:

- *dotted whole note*

- *dotted half note*

---

3. *Ties may be used over bar lines (see Chapter 4, page 32).*
4. *Dots are not used to extend durational values over bar lines.*

- *dotted quarter note*   ♩. = ♩‿♪

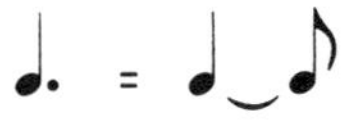

- *dotted eighth note*   ♪. = ♪‿♬

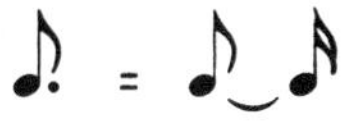

- *dotted sixteenth note*   ♬. = ♬‿♭

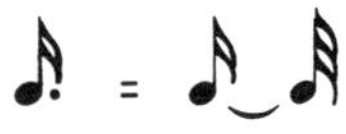

When two dots are used, one beside the other, the durational value of the second dot is half that of the first.

𝅝.. = 𝅝‿♩‿♩   ♩.. = ♩‿♪‿♬

♩.. = ♩‿♩‿♪   ♪.. = ♪‿♬‿♭

Observe that when a dotted or double-dotted note is represented by a tie or ties, the tied notes are written in order of decreasing duration.

RESTS

Rests are symbols for silence in music and are comparable in durational value to notes.

- *whole rest*

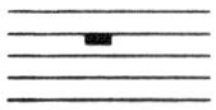

- *half rest*

- *quarter rest*   𝄽

- *eighth rest*   𝄾

- *sixteenth rest*   𝄿

- *thirty-second rest*   𝅀

Notice that, when written on the **staff** (Chapter 3), the whole rest is placed below the fourth line, the half rest above the third line.

Dots are sometimes added to rests just as they are to notes. Some durational equivalents of dotted notes and dotted rests are:

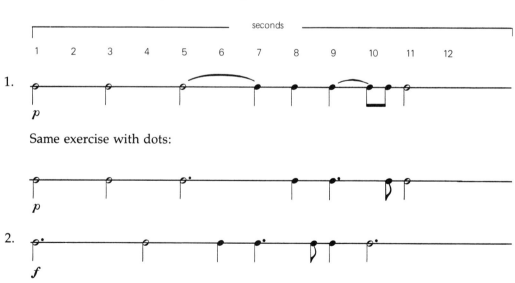

When a dotted or double-dotted note is represented by two or three rests, the rests are written in order of decreasing duration.

2.3 Reading Exercises: Ties, Dots, and Rests

Sing the following. ○ = four seconds.

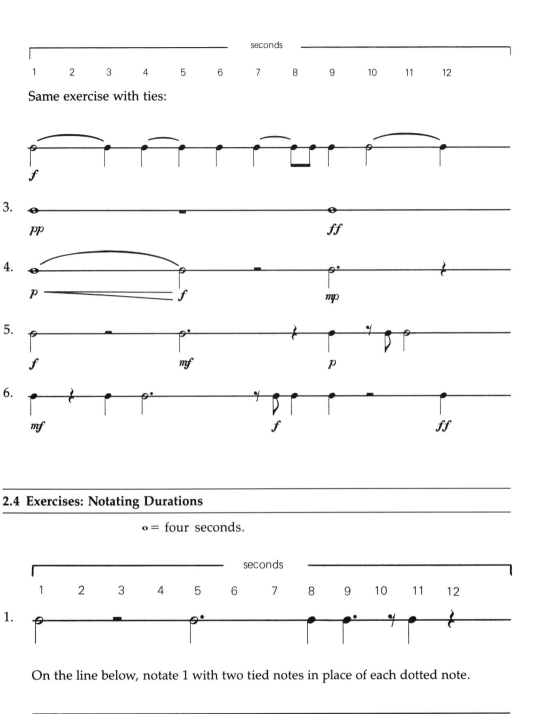

Same exercise with ties:

3.

4.

5.

6.

2.4 Exercises: Notating Durations

𝅝 = four seconds.

1.

On the line below, notate 1 with two tied notes in place of each dotted note.

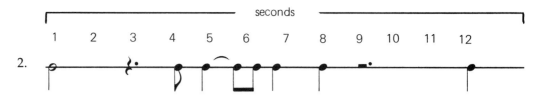

2.

On the line below, notate 2 with two rests in place of each dotted rest.

3.

On the line below, notate 3 with one dotted note in place of each pair of tied notes.

4.

On the line below, notate 4 with one dotted rest in place of each pair of rests.

2.5 Exercises: Calculating Durational Equivalents

1. How many of the designated durations are equivalent to the given note or rest?

Example: ♩⌣♪ = _6_ sixteenth notes

a. 𝅘𝅥𝅮.   = ___ sixteenth notes

b. 𝅗𝅥 ⌣ 𝅘𝅥𝅮 = ___ eighth notes

c. 𝅘𝅥 ⌣ 𝅘𝅥𝅯 = ___ sixteenth notes

d. ═▬.   = ___ quarter rests

e. 𝅘𝅥..   = ___ sixteenth notes

f. 𝅗𝅥.   = ___ eighth notes

g. 𝅝.   = ___ half notes

h. 𝄿.   = ___ sixteenth rests

i. 𝅗𝅥 ⌣ 𝅘𝅥. = ___ eighth notes

j. 𝄾   = ___ sixteenth rests

2. Rewrite as *two* tied notes.

   Example: 𝅘𝅥. = 𝅘𝅥 ⌣ 𝅘𝅥𝅮

   a. 𝅗𝅥. =

   b. 𝅝 =

   c. 𝅘𝅥.. =

   d. 𝅘𝅥 =

   e. 𝅘𝅥𝅮. =

   f. 𝅗𝅥.. =

3. Rewrite as *one* dotted or double-dotted note.

Example: ♩ ‿ ♪ = ♩.

a. ♩ ‿ ♩ ‿ ♩ =

d. ♩ ‿ ♩ =

b. ♩ ‿ ♩ ‿ ♪ =

e. ♪ ‿ ♪ ‿ ♪ =

c. ♩ ‿ ♩ ‿ ♩ =

f. ♪ ‿ ♪ =

PIANO EXERCISES

Use any pitch or pitches on the piano keyboard for the following exercises.

1. Play Exercises 2.1.(a)–(c).

2. Play Exercise 2.1.2(b).

3. With another person play Exercise 2.1.3.

4. Play Exercises 2.3.1–3.

3

Pitch

STAFF

In Chapter 1 lower and higher pitches were represented below and above a single horizontal line. In actual practice, pitch is notated on a **staff**, which consists of five parallel lines and four intervening spaces. The lines and spaces are numbered from bottom to top, from lower to higher pitch.

The staff may be extended with **ledger lines** (also spelled *leger lines*) placed above and below the staff. As with the staff proper, both the ledger lines and the spaces between represent pitches.

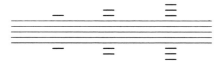

Ledger lines are never connected to one another, and notes in spaces immediately above or below the staff do not require ledger lines.

A note is "in" a space if it fills the space, the outline of the note touching the surrounding staff lines: ⎯𝒐⎯. A note is "on" a line if the line runs through the center of the note, the extremities of the note extending to the center of the surrounding spaces: ⎯𝒐⎯.

When writing stemmed notes on the staff, the practice is to point stems downward when noteheads are on the third line or above, and to extend stems upward when noteheads are below the third line. This consolidates the reading area.

When a group of notes is connected by a beam or beams, the note farthest from the third line determines the direction of the stems. The slant of the beam gives the general direction of the notes' pitches.

CLEF

Only seven letters of the alphabet, *A*, *B*, *C*, *D*, *E*, *F*, and *G*, are required to designate on the staff notes representing the entire pitch range used in Western music. A more specific portion of the pitch range is established by the use of a **clef**. There are three clefs in use; in design they are medieval forms of the letters *G*, *F*, and *C*.

G Clef

The **G clef** or **treble clef** (𝄞), which represents roughly the upper half of the pitch spectrum, establishes G on the second line of the staff. This pitch is within a comfortable singing range for women's voices.

The other lines and spaces are named in ascending order as follows:

In reverse order from G the other lines and spaces are similarly named. The C immediately below the staff is referred to as **middle C**.

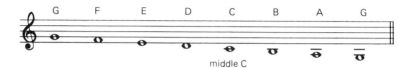

Learning to translate the pitches written on the staff into actual sounds is conveniently done by playing them on the piano keyboard. The keyboard is made up of white keys and black keys, the latter divided into groups of two and three. These recurring patterns of keys are reference points in locating pitches by letter name. The pitches presented above may now be seen with reference to the keyboard.

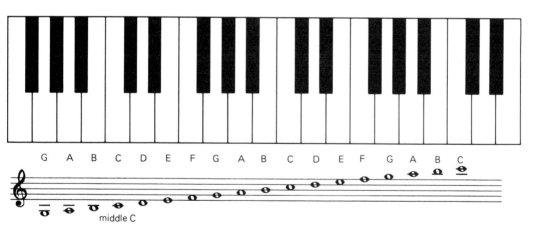

Note that each letter name recurs at a similar place in the black-and-white-key pattern. Middle C is approximately in the center of the keyboard.

The treble clef is used on the upper staff in piano music and to notate music for female voices and instruments of higher pitch such as the violin, flute, trumpet, and xylophone.

3.1 Exercises: Treble Staff

1. Practice drawing the treble clef using the given clef as a model.

2. Commit to memory the letter names of lines and spaces of the treble staff to the second ledger line above and below the staff.

3. Give the letter names of the following pitches.

4. In whole notes, write the pitches indicated.

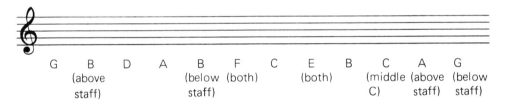

G	B	D	A	B	F	C	E	B	C	A	G
	(above			(below	(both)		(both)		(middle	(above	(below
	staff)			staff)					C)	staff)	staff)

5. On the staff notate a portion of a well-known tune from the pitches and durations given. Allow about a quarter inch between notes. The first note is given. Write the subsequent pitches closest to it.

Find the pitches on the keyboard. What is the tune?

F Clef

The **F clef** or **bass clef** (𝄢), representing approximately the lower half of the pitch spectrum, establishes F on the fourth line of the staff. This pitch is within a comfortable range for the male voice.

Lines and spaces above F are named in ascending order, and below F in reverse order. The C above the bass staff is middle C.

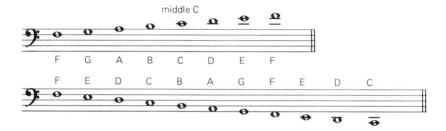

With reference to the keyboard the pitches of the bass staff are:

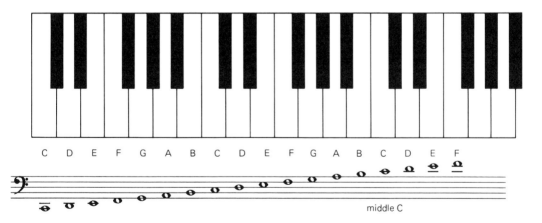

The bass clef is used on the lower staff in piano music and to notate music for low male voices and such instruments as the cello, double bass, bassoon, trombone, and tuba.

3.2 Exercises: Bass Staff

1. Practice drawing the bass clef using the given clef as a model.

2. Commit to memory the letter names of lines and spaces of the bass staff to the second ledger line above and below the staff.

3. Give the letter names of the following pitches.

4. In whole notes write the pitches indicated.

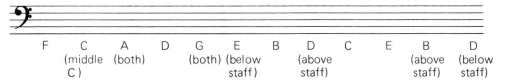

F	C	A	D	G	E	B	D	C	E	B	D
	(middle C)	(both)		(both)	(below staff)		(above staff)			(above staff)	(below staff)

5. On the staff notate a portion of a well-known tune from the pitches and durations given. Allow about a quarter inch between notes. The first note is given. Write the subsequent pitches closest to it.

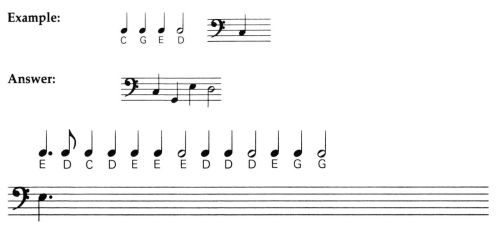

Find the pitches on the keyboard. What is the tune?

C Clef

The **C clef** (𝄡) is a movable clef representing roughly the mid-range of the pitch spectrum and establishes the location of middle C, a pitch within the singing range of both men and women. Today only two of these locations are consistently used: on the third line of the staff, for the **alto clef**, and on the fourth line, for the **tenor clef**.

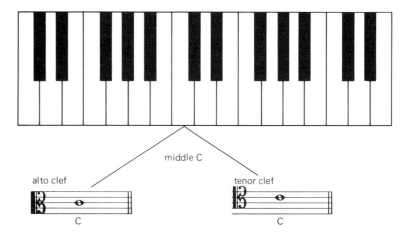

The alto clef is used for notating the music of the viola since it makes the staff most closely correspond to the pitch range of the instrument. Similarly, bass-clef instruments such as the cello, bassoon, and trombone may be called upon to read tenor clef in order to avoid using ledger lines when the pitch range or **tessitura** of the music is high.

GRAND STAFF

When the treble and bass staves are placed one above the other, the treble staff above the bass (in position as well as pitch), and are linked by a bar and brace, they form a **grand staff** or *great staff*.

The grand staff is used for the notation of keyboard music and is useful for the representation of a wide range of pitches. The pitches of the grand staff may now be seen with reference to the central portion of the keyboard.

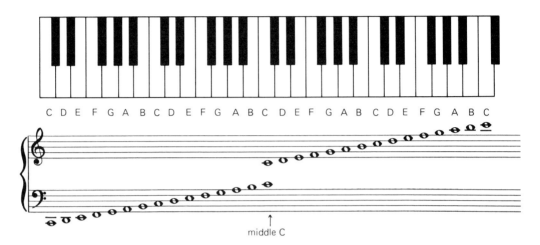

middle C

OCTAVE

As only seven letters of the alphabet are required to name all eighty-eight keys of the piano, there is obviously duplication of letter names. An **octave** is the distance from one C to the next C, from one D to the next D, and so on. The octave results from doubling or halving the frequency of vibration of a sounding body. The first A above middle C, to which orchestras tune, vibrates at a frequency of 440 vibrations per second. An octave below this has a vibration rate of 220 and an octave above of 880.

To facilitate reading the pitches notated on ledger lines, an **octave sign** may be used. This is an 8 followed by a dotted line, signifying an octave higher if placed above the staff, an octave lower if placed below the staff.[1] The dotted line encompasses the notes included in the octave placement.

---

1. *8ve and 8va are also used and have the same meaning.*

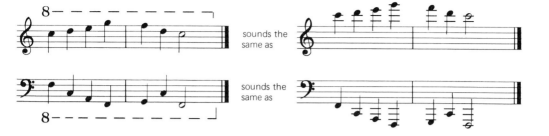

sounds the same as

sounds the same as

CHAPTER EXERCISES

1. On the grand staff below:
    a. Add stems to the note heads and beam in groups of two eighth notes.
    b. Disregarding pitch, read aloud the letter names of the notes at a speed at which you are able to maintain equal durations. Read several times, increasing the speed as you gain facility.

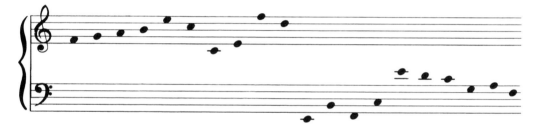

2. On the grand staff below:
    a. Add stems to the note heads and beam in groups of four sixteenth notes.
    b. Read aloud as in Exercise 1(b).

3. Rewrite these notes on the treble, alto, and tenor staves so that they will sound at the *same* pitches.

   Example:

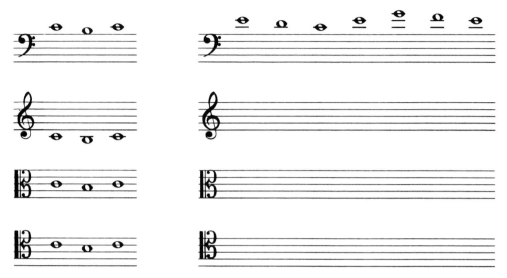

   a. Find the pitches on the keyboard and match them with your voice. Sing the letter names.
   b. Repeat (a) until you are able to sing the pitches with equal durations and without the keyboard.
   c. Sing, reading each clef separately.

4. Rewrite these notes on the bass staff so that they will sound at the same pitches.

   Example:

   a. Find the pitches on the keyboard and match them with your voice. Sing the letter names.
   b. Repeat (a) until you are able to sing the pitches with appropriate durations (♩ = one second).

5. Rewrite the following notes as indicated.

   a. Rewrite the bass notes *one* octave higher on the treble staff. The first three notes are given as an example.

   b. Rewrite the treble notes *one* octave lower on the bass staff. The first three notes are given.

   c. Rewrite the bass notes *two* octaves higher on the treble staff. The first three notes are given.

   d. Rewrite the treble notes *three* octaves lower on the bass staff. The first three notes are given.

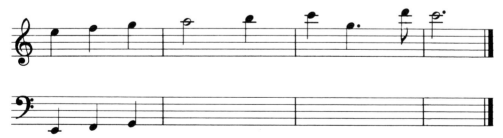

PIANO EXERCISES

1. Find middle C on the piano keyboard.

2. With the right hand play the pitches from the illustrations of the treble staff (page 21).

3. Find on the keyboard the pitches in Exercise 3.1.3.

4. With the left hand play the pitches from the illustrations of the bass staff (page 23).

5. Find on the keyboard the pitches in Exercise 3.2.3.

6. Play the pitches from the illustration of the grand staff (page 26).

4

Beat, Meter, Rhythm

BEAT

There is an underlying pulse that persists from the beginning to the end of almost all music. It is to this that one reacts physically when hearing or participating in marches or dances. The pulse, plus the time span between one pulse and the next, constitute the **beat**.

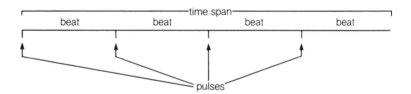

A single beat is represented by a note. A frequent choice, for example, is the quarter note, which in a series of beats would appear like this: ♩ ♩ ♩ ♩ ♩ and so on. Among other possibilities are half-note beats, ♩ ♩ ♩ ♩ ♩, or eighth-note beats, ♪ ♪ ♪ ♪ ♪.

With reference to the marches and dances mentioned above, pulses recur regularly but are unequal in strength. Thus beats represented by quarter notes may succeed each other as follows, the accent mark signifying a stronger pulse.

- *in marches*

- *in waltzes*

- *in some marches, dances, and songs*

In the last example the smaller accent is a less strong pulse than the larger accent.

METER

When beats are grouped in patterns **meter** exists. One metric pattern usually recurs constantly in a short musical composition. The patterns in the three previous examples are identified specifically as:

- *duple meter, two beats in an accented-unaccented pattern:*

- *triple meter, three beats in a pattern of one accented plus two unaccented beats:*

- *quadruple meter, four beats in a pattern of one accented beat, one unaccented beat, one beat with a secondary accent, and another unaccented beat:*

MEASURES, BAR LINES

Each metric pattern is completed within a period of time called a **measure**. One measure is separated from another by a **bar line**. A **double bar line** signals the end of a section or composition.

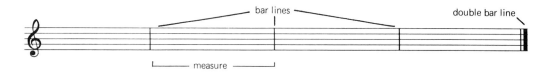

METER SIGNATURES

The first sign to appear on a staff is the clef sign, which gives pitch orientation. Following this is a **meter signature**, sometimes called the *time signature*, which denotes the metric pattern to be used. The meter signature consists of two numbers in vertical alignment above and below the middle line of the staff, the lower number indicating the *type of note* representing one beat (for example, 2 = 𝅗𝅥, 4 = ♩, 8 = ♪), the upper number indicating the *number of beats* in each measure.

Although others are possible, the most frequently used duple, triple, and quadruple meter signatures are:

- *duple*

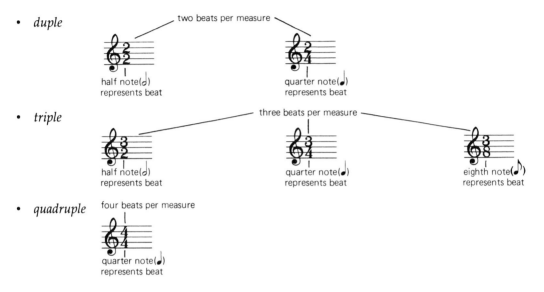

- *triple*

- *quadruple*

4.1 Exercises: Meter Signatures

1. Write on the staves the meter signatures indicated.

   Example: a duple meter in which the beat is represented by a quarter note

   a. a triple meter in which the beat is represented by an eighth note

   b. a duple meter in which the beat is represented by a half note

c. a triple meter in which the beat is represented by a quarter note

d. a quadruple meter in which the beat is represented by a quarter note

e. a triple meter in which the beat is represented by a half note

2. Describe the following, less frequently used meter signatures.

Example: $\frac{4}{8}$ There are four beats per measure and the eighth note represents the beat.

a. $\frac{4}{2}$ b. $\frac{3}{1}$ c. $\frac{4}{16}$ d. $\frac{2}{8}$

TEMPO AND TEMPO MARKINGS

Since values of notes are relative to one another and do not have fixed time spans, a suggestion must be given as to the rate of speed at which beats recur. This rate of speed is called **tempo** and is indicated by **tempo markings** written above the staff at the beginning of the composition. These markings are usually Italian words, although English, French, and German words may be used instead. Some of them are:

- *largo*   slow and stately (the slowest marking)
- *lento*   slow (between largo and andante)
- *adagio*   slow
- *andante*   moderately slow, easily flowing
- *moderato*   at a moderate tempo
- *allegro*   lively, brisk, rapid
- *presto*   fast, rapid (faster than allegro)

Tempos are more precisely indicated by *metronome markings*. A **metronome** is a mechanical apparatus the function of which is to sound beats at regular intervals. If the metronome marking is M.M. ♩ = 60[1] (which means that the quarter note recurs at a rate of sixty per minute) the tempo is slow, and if M.M. ♩ = 208 it is fast. The approximate tempo for marching is M.M. ♩ = 120, or two steps per second.

SIMPLE METER

A meter in which the beat naturally divides into multiples of two is called **simple meter**.

Following are the most frequently used simple meters. Each note represents a beat and each example constitutes one measure.

- *simple duple meter*
- *simple triple meter*
- *simple quadruple meter*

4.2 Exercises: Simple Meter

Perform the above one-measure examples as follows.

1. Establish a tempo (for example, M.M. beat = 120) by tapping the foot.

2. Intone the beat numbers with characteristic metric accentuation, repeating until each example can be performed with fluency (for example, õne two, õne two, and so on).

3. Keep your eyes on the example being performed so that the notation becomes associated with the sound.

---

1. **M.M.** *means Maelzel's metronome, and refers to the man regarded as the inventor. The letters M.M. are not always included in a tempo marking.*

CONDUCTING

Conducting is the physical act of directing a performing group. Certain gestures by the conductor to indicate metric patterns have become traditional. Two gestures that are standard for all meters are a strong downward movement of the arm for the first beat of the measure, called the **downbeat**, and an upward movement for the final beat of the measure, called the **upbeat**. At the beginning of a performance one beat of preparation is given to establish tempo. The following patterns are from the conductor's point of view.

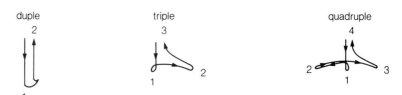

4.3 Exercises: Conducting

1. At a tempo of beat = 120, practice conducting in duple, triple, and quadruple meters. Begin with an upbeat and maintain a steady tempo.

2. Conduct the metric patterns of pieces played by the instructor.

RHYTHM IN SIMPLE METER

Rarely does music consist entirely of notes equal in duration to the beat itself. Instead, music proceeds with a variety of durations (notes and rests)—some equal to the beat, some shorter than the beat, and some longer than the beat. This diversity of durations, together with the implications of meter, is called **rhythm**.[2]

In a measure the totals of the durations and of the implied beats are the same.

---

2. *Appendix A contains a syllable system for rhythmic reading that may be used in this chapter and throughout the book.*

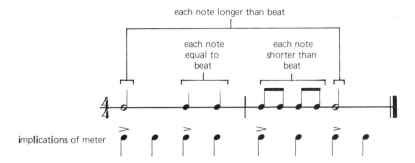

each note longer than beat

each note equal to beat

each note shorter than beat

implications of meter

DURATIONS SHORTER THAN THE BEAT

Durations shorter than the beat are represented by *divisions* or *subdivisions* of the beat unit. The most frequently used beat units in simple meter are shown next with their divisions and subdivisions.

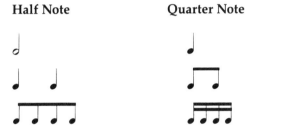

	Half Note	**Quarter Note**	**Eighth Note**
• *beat*			
• *division*			
• *subdivision*			

Following are the simple meters discussed previously with one-measure examples illustrating beats, divisions, and subdivisions.

• *simple duple meter*

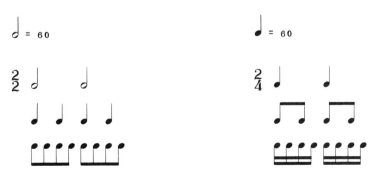

- *simple triple meter*

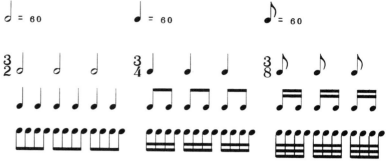

- *simple quadruple meter*

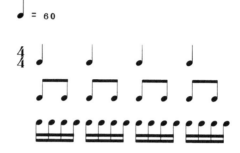

Except in division where the half note is the beat unit, divisions and subdivisions are beamed so that the metric organization within a measure is clear.

Examples:

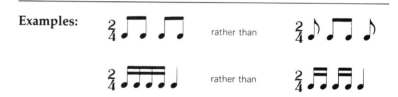

4.4 Exercise: Durations Shorter than the Beat

1. With the class divided into three groups, perform each of the duple, triple, and quadruple one-measure examples above as indicated.

   Group I taps a steady beat with the foot while intoning the beat numbers.

Group II claps the division of the beat.

Group III taps the subdivision of the beat on desks with pencils or knuckles.

With characteristic metric accentuation repeat these one-measure patterns until they can be performed with fluency.

DURATIONS LONGER THAN THE BEAT

A duration longer than the beat is notated in one or more of the following ways:

- *by writing a single note value that combines beats*

- *by using dotted notes*

- *by using ties (durations that extend over the bar line must use the tie)*

Below are meters with a single duration that constitutes a full measure.

- *simple duple meter* $\frac{2}{2}$ 𝅝 $\frac{2}{4}$ 𝅗𝅥

- *simple triple meter* $\frac{3}{2}$ 𝅝. $\frac{3}{4}$ 𝅗𝅥. $\frac{3}{8}$ ♩.

- *simple quadruple meter* $\frac{4}{4}$ 𝅝

A full measure of silence in *any* meter is indicated by a whole rest.

1. In the above meters and at a tempo of beat = 100, sing and sustain any pitch for a full measure. Repeat while conducting.

THE QUARTER NOTE AS BEAT UNIT

The quarter note most frequently serves as the beat unit, for two reasons.

1. It is in the middle range of note values and thus most easily allows representation of durations longer and shorter than the beat.

    For example, if the beat were 𝅝, longer durations would be awkward. If the beat were ♪, division and subdivision would be difficult to comprehend readily.

2. At the division level, the reading of rhythm is facilitated by the use of beams to connect groups of notes. Compare the two illustrations below, one with quarter note as beat, the other with half note as beat. The three beamed groups in the first illustration immediately identify the beats, whereas the unbeamed notes in the second illustration show no groupings.

    At the subdivision level, on the other hand, the first illustration below is easier to read than the second illustration, where extra beaming is required.

SONGS IN SIMPLE METER

Here are excerpts from three well-known songs. Implied beats are shown below the staff. Accent marks are not needed on the staff to show metric organization, as strong and weak pulses are implied by the meter signatures. With regard to rhythm, some note values coincide with the beat and some note values are longer or shorter than the beat. Tempo and dynamic markings are indicated above the staff and the text is printed below.

1. duple meter

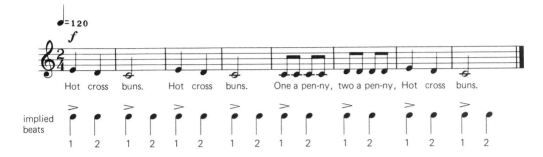

2. triple meter

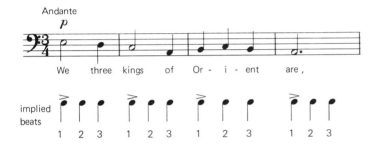

3. quadruple meter

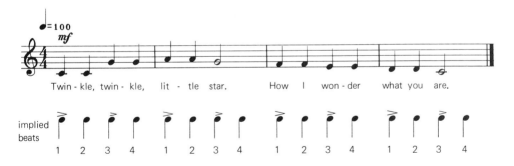

4.6 Exercises: Songs in Simple Meter

Do the following exercises for each of the songs above.

1. Count aloud the implied beats, placing emphasis where appropriate and maintaining a steady tempo.

2. Speak the words in the notated rhythm and tap the beats.

3. Find the pitches on the keyboard and match the pitches with your voice. Change octave if necessary.

4. Sing the song with words at the established tempo and dynamic level while keeping your eyes on the music. Your voice provides the timbre.

5. Practice conducting the song.

COMMON TIME AND ALLA BREVE

Two time signatures that are relics of former systems of notation but still in use today are 𝄴, which signifies **common time**, the equivalent of $\frac{4}{4}$ time, and 𝄵, the symbol for **alla breve** or **cut time**, the equivalent of $\frac{2}{2}$ time.

Examples:

4.7 Exercises: Common Time and Alla Breve

Do the following exercises for each of the songs above.

1. Count the implied beats aloud, placing emphasis where appropriate and maintaining a steady tempo.

2. Speak the words in the notated rhythm.

3. Find the pitches on the keyboard and match the pitches with your voice. Change octave if necessary.

4. Sing the song with words at the established tempo and dynamic level while keeping your eyes on the music.

5. Practice conducting the song.

UPBEAT OR ANACRUSIS

A piece of music does not always begin with the first beat of the measure. It may begin with one or more unaccented notes, and if so the first bar line appears just before the primary accent of the first complete measure. This unaccented beginning is the **upbeat** or **anacrusis**. The final measure of the composition will traditionally be incomplete, and when added to the upbeat will total one complete measure.

"My Bonnie Lies over the Ocean," for example, begins on an unaccented beat. The final measure has a duration equal to two beats.

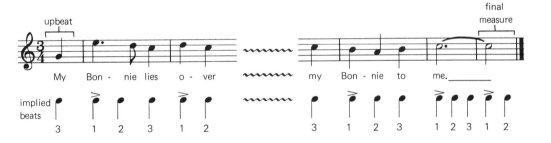

CHAPTER EXERCISES

1. Rewrite the following with, where appropriate, beams in place of flags.

Example:

a.

b.

c.

d.

e.

f.

2. Add bar lines to the following. A bar line already present is preceded by an anacrusis.

3. Where a bracket occurs add one note to complete the measure.

Example:

Answer:

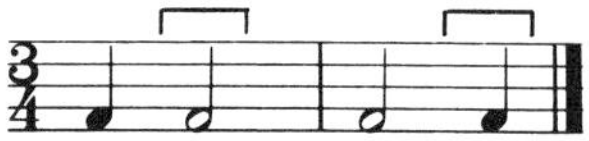

a.

b.

c.

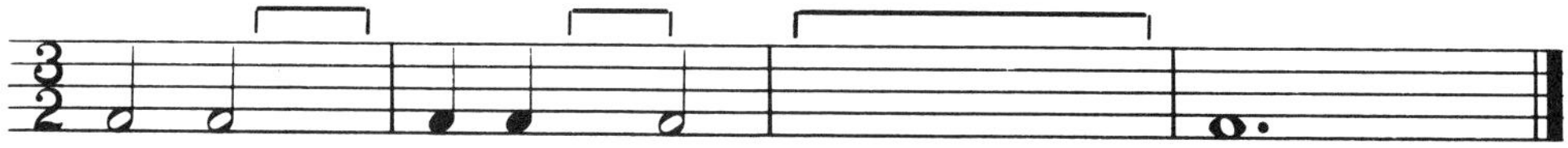

d.

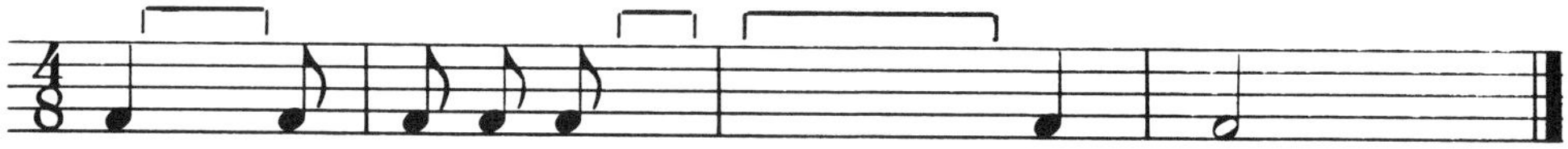

e.

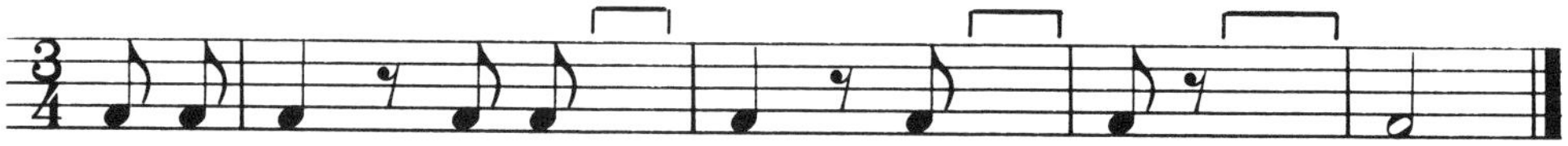

f.

g.

h.

4. Where a bracket occurs add one rest to complete the measure.
   Make whole rests like this:    Make half rests like this:

Example:

Answer:

5. Add meter signatures to the following.

Example: **Answer:**

c.

d.

e.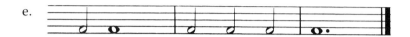

f.

g.

h.

6. At a tempo of beat = 80, practice the following rhythm exercises until each can be performed fluently. Maintain a steady beat and use rhythmic syllables.

a.

b.

c.

d.

e.

f.

7. Rhythmic duets for additional practice.
   Instructor: Begin by practicing each part separately. Sing as duets at an interval of a perfect fifth.

PIANO EXERCISES

1. Play the excerpts from "Hot Cross Buns," "We Three Kings," "Twinkle, Twinkle, Little Star," "Au clair de la lune," and "Yankee Doodle" (pages 41–42).[3]

2. Using any pitch on the keyboard, play Exercise 6 of the Chapter Exercises.

3. With another person, play Exercise 7 of the Chapter Exercises.

_____

3. *Appendix C contains information on piano fingering and on playing melodies.*

5

Rhythm, *Continued*

DIVISION AND SUBDIVISION COMBINED

In the previous chapter, one-beat units resulting from division and subdivision were illustrated. Other one-beat units result from combining division and subdivision.

Example: Quarter Note (♩) as Beat

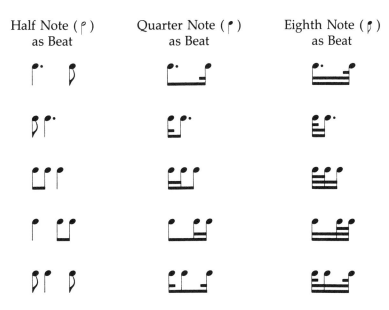

Half Note (𝅗𝅥) as Beat   Quarter Note (♩) as Beat   Eighth Note (♪) as Beat

5.1 Exercise: Division and Subdivision Combined

1. At a tempo of beat = 100, repeat each of the one-beat units above with a neutral syllable and pitch until the rhythm becomes familiar. Keep your eyes on the page so that the representation of the one-beat unit and its sound become integrated.

ILLUSTRATIONS OF RHYTHM

In a piece of music, rhythm units (one-beat units or durations longer than the beat) move forward in a continuous rhythmic flow. Only a few different rhythm units are present in any one piece. They recur, however, and together with the tempo give a composition its unique and recognizable rhythmic character.

Following are song excerpts showing rhythm units discussed in this and the previous chapter. Notice the recurrence of each song's characteristic rhythm units.

1. longer than the beat

2. equal to the beat

Beethoven, Ninth Symphony

3. divided beat

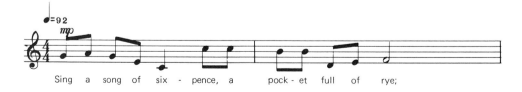

4. subdivided beat

Knock, knock! An-y- bod-y there? Come in-to the sun -light, see who's here.

5. division and subdivision combined

Mine eyes have seen the glo - ry of the com - ing of the Lord;

If a bo- dy meet a bo - dy com - in' through the rye

What shall we do with a drunk - en sail - or, What shall we do with a drunk - en sail - or,

Jim - my crack corn and I don't care, Jim - my crack corn and I don't care,

---

5.2 Exercise: Recurrence of Rhythm Units

---

1. Perform each of the above excerpts at the given tempo by intoning the words while conducting.

TRIPLET

A **triplet** is a three-note group resulting from irregular division of a note that may serve as a simple beat. Triplets are recognized by a 3 written at the stem end of the group.

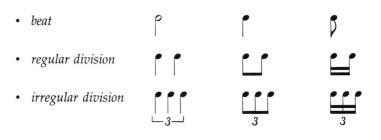

- *beat*
- *regular division*
- *irregular division*

Examples:

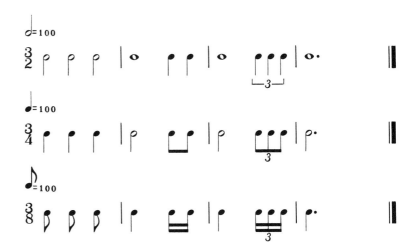

5.3 Exercises: Triplets in Simple Triple Meter

1. With two groups perform the above triplet examples as follows.

   Group I taps a steady beat while intoning beat numbers.
   Group II sings on a neutral pitch and syllable.

   Repeat until fluent. Note that all three examples sound identical.

2. Perform the following measures by conducting a steady beat while intoning the words at the tempo and dynamic level indicated.

Notice the rhythmic fluency of the three syllables of "beau-ti-ful" when rendered with a triplet.

SYNCOPATION

Syncopation can occur at several durational levels in relation to the beat. It results when a note is initiated on a weak beat or between pulses and is given emphasis either by extending its duration over the next pulse or by the use of an accent mark.

In the illustration below, the second beat (weak) extends over the third beat (strong) and by its duration receives more emphasis.[1] The syncopated note is marked with an arrow.

Similarly, the second note of a division receives more emphasis when it extends over the pulse that follows,

and the second note of a subdivision receives more emphasis when it extends over the division that follows.

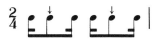

---

1. *Durational emphasis is called **agogic accent**.*

A contrasting intensity level for the syncopated note may strengthen its effect.

5.4 Exercises: Syncopation

1. Practice the above one-measure examples of syncopation until they can be performed with fluency.

2. Below are portions of songs that include syncopation. In each excerpt the syncopated note is indicated with an arrow. Intone the words on a neutral pitch while tapping the beat.

a.

Moderato

My Lord, what a morn - ing, My Lord, what a morn - ing,

b.

Allegro

De la Sie - rra Mo - re - na, Cie - li - to

Lin - do, vie - nen ba - jan - do,_____

c.

Lit - tle Da - vid, play on your harp, Hal - le - lu! Hal - le - lu!

d.

In Dub - lin's fair cit - y, Where girls are so pret - ty,

RHYTHM PATTERNS

In music such as folk songs, rhythm units tend to fall into rhythm patterns one to four measures long. Patterns are often immediately repeated either exactly or with slight modification. Silence, represented by rests, is intrinsic to some patterns.

Here, portions of several songs illustrate rhythm patterns and their repetitions.

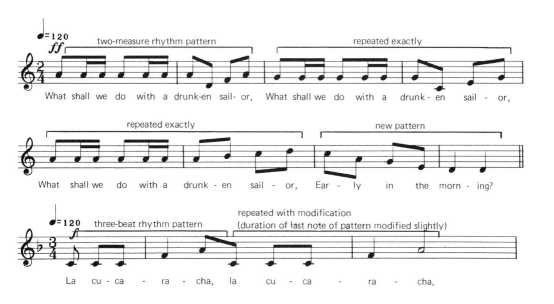

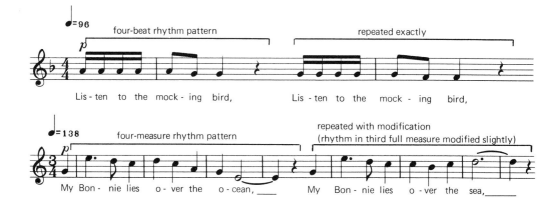

RHYTHM AND WORDS

Notice in the previous examples that syllables emphasized in speaking receive the same metric emphasis in rhythmic notation.

Examples:

- *from "Drunken Sailor"*

- *from "Listen to the Mocking Bird"*

- *from "My Bonnie Lies over the Ocean"*

5.5 Exercise: Rhythm and Words

Below are rhythm patterns, one each in duple, triple, and quadruple meter. Add meter signatures and bar lines so that the metric emphasis of the notation and the emphasis of the words coincide.

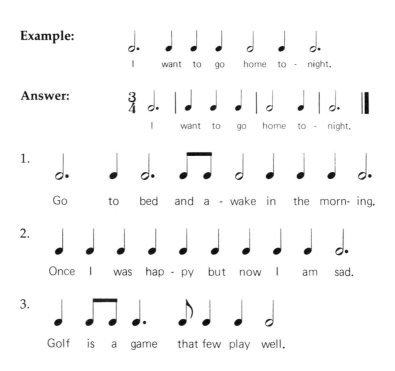

Example:

I want to go home to - night.

Answer:

I want to go home to - night.

1. Go to bed and a - wake in the morn- ing.

2. Once I was hap - py but now I am sad.

3. Golf is a game that few play well.

CHAPTER EXERCISES

1. Where a bracket occurs, add one note or two tied notes to illustrate a duration longer than a beat.

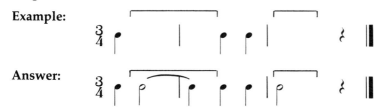

Example:

Answer:

a.

b.

c.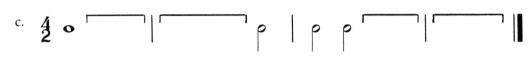

d.

e.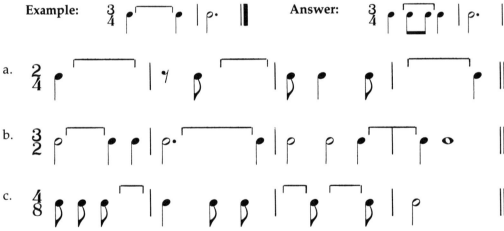

2. Where a bracket occurs, add two notes to illustrate beat division.

Example: $\frac{3}{4}$ ♩ ♩ | ♩. ‖ **Answer:** $\frac{3}{4}$ ♩ ♪♪♩ | ♩. ‖

a. $\frac{2}{4}$

b. $\frac{3}{2}$

c. $\frac{4}{8}$

d. $\frac{3}{4}$

e. $\frac{4}{4}$

3. Where a bracket occurs, complete the beat to illustrate beat subdivision.

Example: 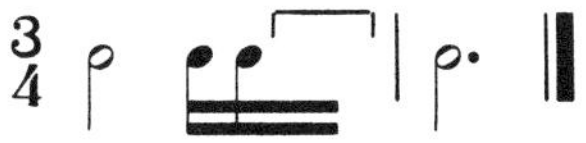 **Answer:**

a.

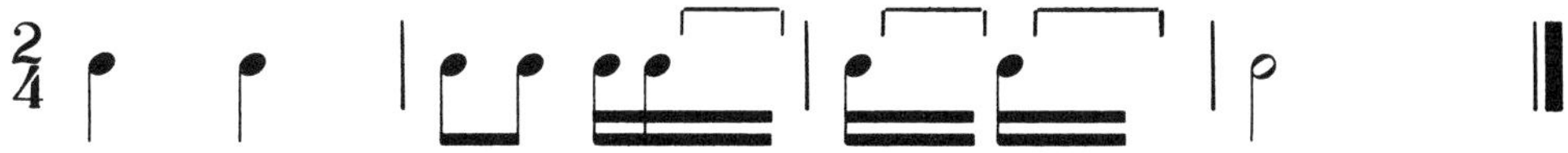

b.

c.

d.

e.

4. Where a bracket occurs, add a one-beat unit to illustrate division and subdivision combined. Use a variety of units.

Example: 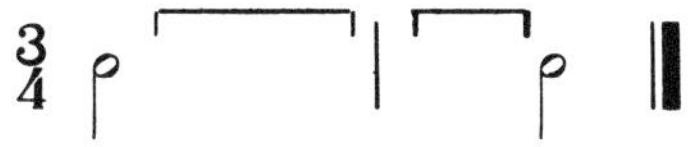 **Answer:**

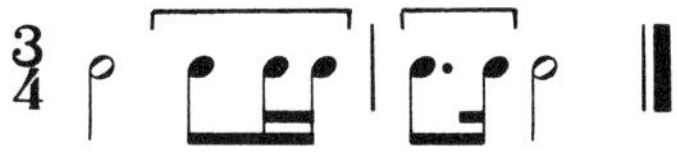

a.

b.

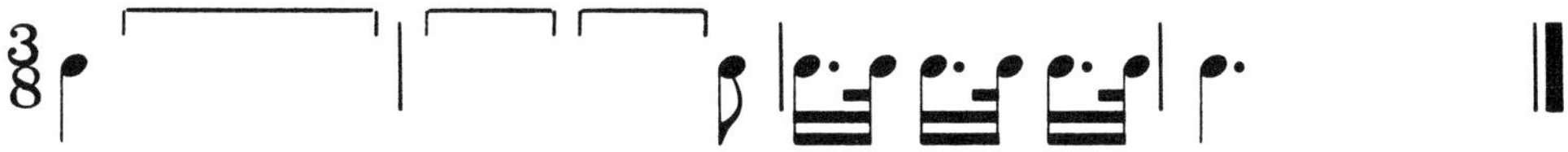

c.

d.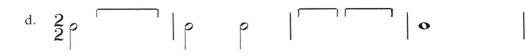

e.

5. Where a bracket occurs, add a triplet.

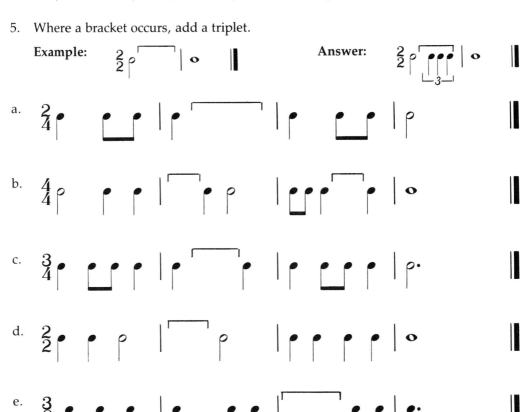

Example: **Answer:**

a.

b.

c.

d.

e.

6. Where a bracket occurs, add one note or two tied notes to illustrate syncopation.

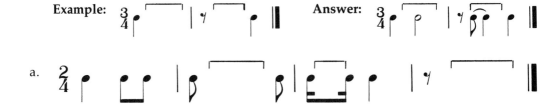

Example: **Answer:**

a.

b.

c.

d.

e.

7. Complete the following measures, illustrating repeating rhythm patterns with slight modification. Words suggest rhythm, and each syllable is represented by a note.

Example:

Come and sing a song to me. Sing a song of love, O!

a.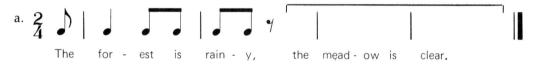

The for - est is rain - y, the mead - ow is clear.

b.

Come to the fair, come and en - joy it. Steal a - way and spend the day.

c.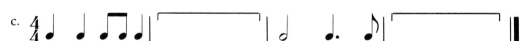

Gin - ger, cin-na-mon, nut-meg, car-da-mon and cloves, cum - in, all - spice.

8. Invent easily singable two-measure rhythm patterns in the following meters and repeat each one with slight modification.

Example:

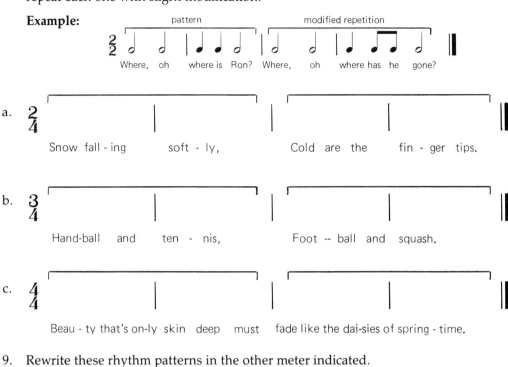

a.

Snow fall - ing   soft - ly,   Cold are the   fin - ger tips.

b.

Hand-ball   and   ten - nis,   Foot -- ball and   squash.

c.

Beau - ty that's on-ly skin deep   must   fade like the dai-sies of spring - time.

9. Rewrite these rhythm patterns in the other meter indicated.

Example:

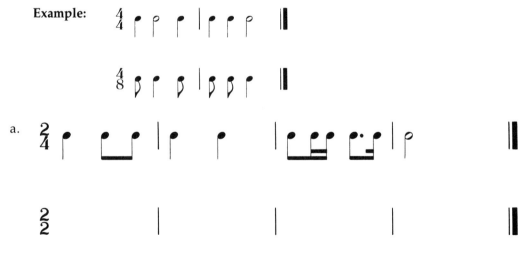

a.

b.

c.

10. Find examples of repeating rhythm patterns in songs.

11. Practice and be able to perform all of the exercises included in 1–9 above.

12. At a tempo of beat = 80, practice the following rhythm exercises until each can be performed fluently. Maintain a steady beat.

a.

b.

c.

d.

e.

f.

13. Rhythmic duets for additional practice.
   Instructor: Begin by practicing each part separately. Sing as **duets at an interval of** a major sixth.

a.

b.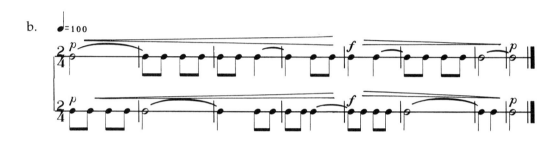

c.

d.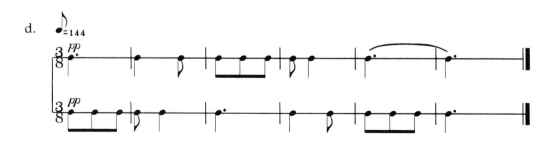

e.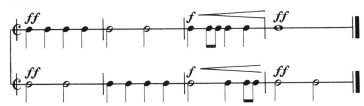

PIANO EXERCISES

1. From "Illustrations of Rhythm" (pages 52–53) play song excerpts 1–4 with correct rhythm.

2. Play Exercise 5.4.2(e).

3. Using any pitch on the keyboard, play Exercise 12 of the Chapter Exercises.

4. With another person, each playing a different pitch, perform Exercise 13 of the Chapter Exercises.

6

Accidentals and the Chromatic Scale

HALF STEP AND WHOLE STEP

Within each octave of the piano keyboard there are seven white and five black keys representing twelve different pitches. The smallest pitch difference traditionally used in Western music is the **half step** or *semitone*. It is the name given to the difference in pitch between one key and its immediate neighbor, that is, between a white key and the preceding or following black key, between a black key and the preceding or following white key, and between the white keys E and F and B and C. A **whole step** is equivalent to two half steps.

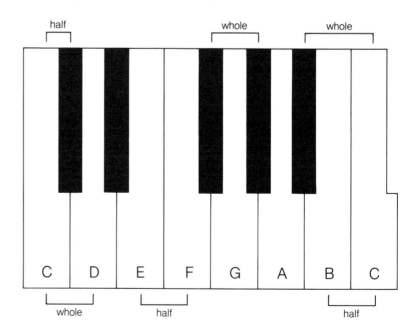

SHARP, FLAT, NATURAL

Because only seven letters of the alphabet are used to name the twelve pitches within the octave, further qualification of pitch names is necessary. For example, the black key immediately following C can be represented as a C that is raised in pitch by a half step, or as a D that is lowered in pitch by a half step. These pitch alterations are indicated by notational symbols called **accidentals**. The three main accidentals are the **sharp**, **flat**, and **natural**.

In notation an accidental is placed immediately before a note. The **sharp** (♯) raises the pitch of the note a half step, the **flat** (♭) lowers its pitch a half step, and the **natural** (♮) cancels a sharp or flat.

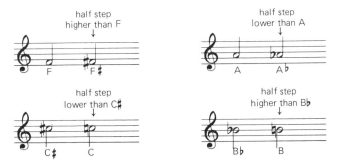

All pitches within the octave may now be identified by letter name and related to the keyboard.

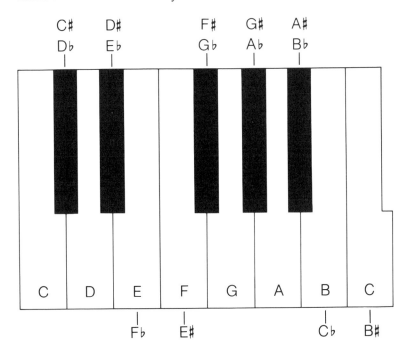

DOUBLE SHARP AND DOUBLE FLAT

The **double sharp** (×) raises the pitch of a note by two half steps, and the **double flat** (♭♭) lowers it by two half steps. If the double sharp or double flat is completely canceled later in a measure, a natural is used to indicate the cancellation.

Partial cancellation is accomplished in either of two ways:

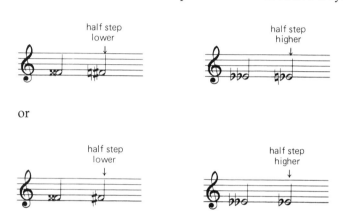

or

ENHARMONIC PITCHES

The illustration on page 69 reveals that one pitch may be notated in more than one way. **Enharmonic** is the term used to refer to different notations of the same pitch—C♯ and D♭, D♯ and E♭, F and E♯, to name a few examples. Double sharps and double flats increase the number of enharmonic possibilities, as shown next.

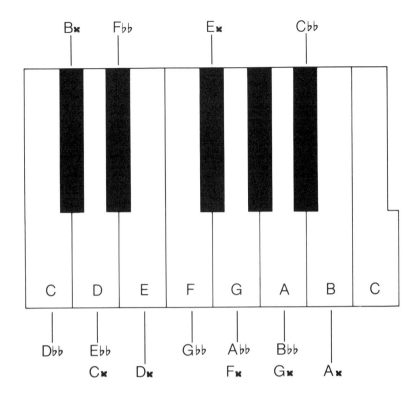

Double flats, double sharps, and enharmonic pitches are rarely encountered by the beginner. However, an understanding of them is necessary in order to appreciate the range of possibilities for pitch notation in Western music.

NOTATING ACCIDENTALS

Six points to remember about accidentals are:

1. An accidental is written on the line or in the space of the note it precedes. In prose it is referred to as in speech—"A-flat" (or "A♭"), "B-natural" ("B♮"), "F-sharp" ("F♯").

2. If a note is made sharp or flat within a measure, that note remains sharp or flat for the duration of the measure and if repeated need not be renotated.

3. If a natural cancels a sharp or flat in a measure, the note remains natural within that measure or until it is made sharp or flat again.

4. A natural is not needed unless a note has previously been made sharp or flat.

5. A bar line cancels the accidentals used in the previous measure.

6. Accidentals apply only to the octave in which they are placed.

CHROMATIC SCALE

Pitch materials of traditional Western music are derived from arrangements of pitches in successive order called **scales**. Most scales consist of seven pitches to the octave, the specific order of whole and half steps determining the scale type. The scale that includes twelve half steps within the octave and thus encompasses the pitch material of all scale types is the **chromatic scale**. Shown below, it illustrates the general tendency to use accidentals that raise pitch if a series of notes moves in an ascending direction, and accidentals that lower pitch if a series of notes moves in a descending direction.

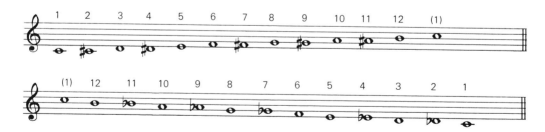

A chromatic scale is rarely used as the basis for an entire composition, but portions are often used for expressive or coloristic effect.

Eve - ning shad - ows creep-ing up the moun-tain Bring me near the time to be with you.

CHAPTER
EXERCISES

1. Locate the notes on the keyboard by placing the number on the appropriate white or black key.

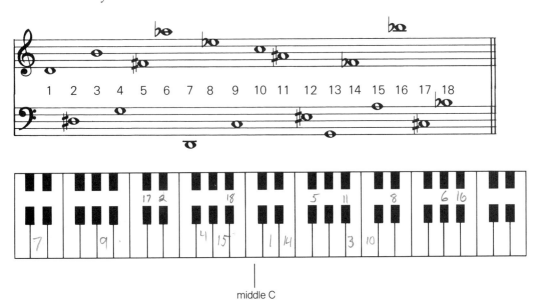

middle C

2. Write a note with a different letter name as indicated.

Example: a half step above the given note.

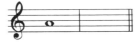

Answer:

a. a half step above the given note[1]

b. a whole step below the given note

c. a half step below the given note

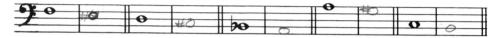

d. a whole step above the given note

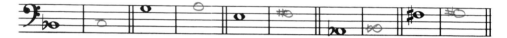

3. By placing accidentals in front of the notes indicated with arrows, complete a chromatic scale (a) on G, (b) on B♭, (c) on E♭, and (d) on D.

Example:

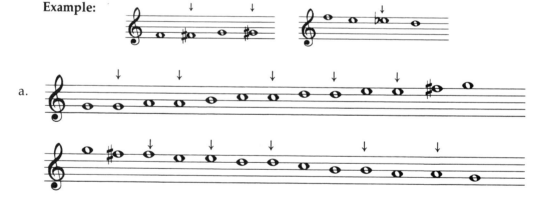

a.

---

1. *Half steps do not* **always** *involve accidentals (see page 68).*

b.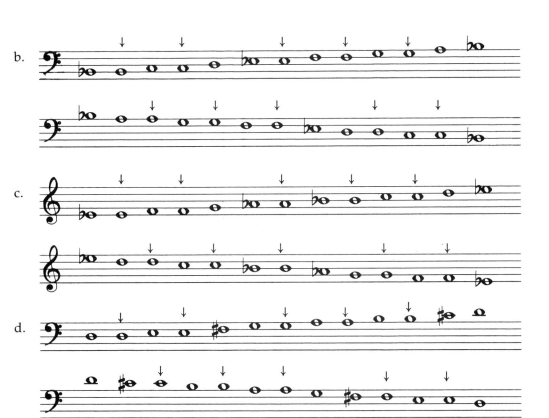

c.

d.

4. Write enharmonic equivalents to the given pitches.

Example: Answer:

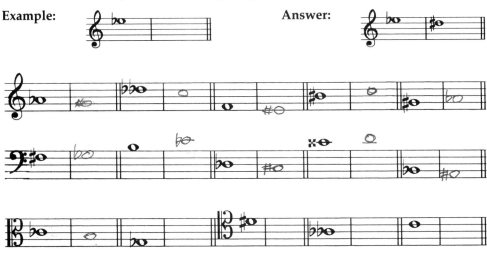

5. The following exercises are designed to develop the ability to distinguish between half and whole steps.

   a. Play and sing these half steps.

   b. Play and sing these whole steps.

   c. Try to distinguish between a half and a whole step when played by another person.

   d. Play one note on the piano or other instrument[2] and match the pitch with your voice. Sing the note a half step above and then return to the first note. Check your pitch with the piano. Do the same with a half step below. Follow the illustration.

   - *half step above*

   - *half step below*

   Repeat the exercise with a whole step, and then repeat the entire exercise on different pitches.

PIANO EXERCISES

1. With the right hand, play the illustration of the chromatic scale (page 72) using the following fingering: 1 3 1 3 1 2 3 1 3 1 3 1 2. Reverse the fingering for the descending scale.

---

2. *On a fretted instrument such as ukulele or guitar each fret represents a half step.*

2. Play the pitches included in Exercise 1 of the Chapter Exercises.

3. Play all of the half and whole steps included in Exercise 2 of the Chapter Exercises.

4. Play the completed chromatic scales in Exercise 3 of the Chapter Exercises.

CHAPTER

7

Major Scales and Key Signatures

MAJOR SCALE[1] There are *seven* seven-tone scales that begin on successive white keys of the piano keyboard. Only *one*, however, from C to C, has the pattern of whole and half steps that identifies it as **major**.

With W for whole step, H for half step, and scale degrees numbered, the major scale pattern is as follows.

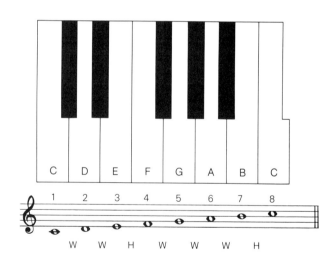

---

1. *Appendix B contains syllable systems for pitch reading that may be used in this chapter and throughout the book.*

A scale is named for the first note, the **tonic** or **keynote**. Above, then, is the scale of C major.

The major scale may begin on any one of the other eleven pitches of the octave. That is, it may be reproduced having any other pitch as tonic while retaining the same sequence of whole and half steps. If the scale begins on F, the fourth degree, B, must be lowered to B♭ to form the half step between scale degrees 3 and 4. If the scale begins on G, the pattern is maintained by raising the seventh note, F, to F♯.

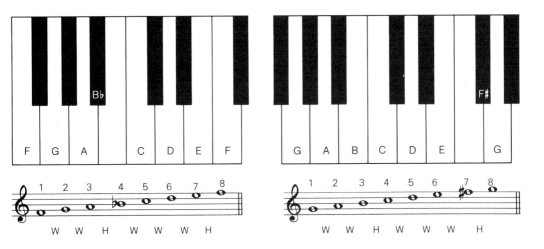

TETRACHORDS

It may be helpful in learning the major scale system to think of the major scale in terms of two four-note scale patterns called **tetrachords**. The two tetrachords, with a whole step between them, are constructed in the identical pattern of W W H and designated lower and upper.

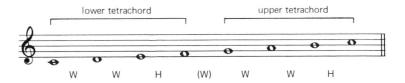

The upper tetrachord of the scale of C major is also the lower tetrachord of the G major scale. Conversely, the lower tetrachord of the scale of C major is also the upper tetrachord of the F major scale.

By extending tetrachords beginning with those of C major, the new tonics for all major scales will be seen to be:

KEY SIGNATURE

The first note of a scale, the keynote or tonic, gives its name to the **key** or **tonality** in which music is written. For example, the scale of C major is said to be *in* the key or tonality of C major. By convention the sharps and flats in a specific key are not written before their respective notes, but are placed immediately after the clef sign, in the order in which they appear in the series of scales, and in that position are referred to as the **key signature**.

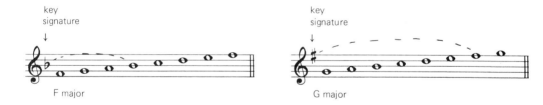

Following are all the major scales, first with sharps and flats written in as accidentals and then with sharps and flats written as key signatures. If a key signature is used, the sharps or flats of that key signature are not written as accidentals in the music itself.

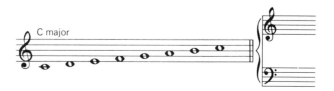

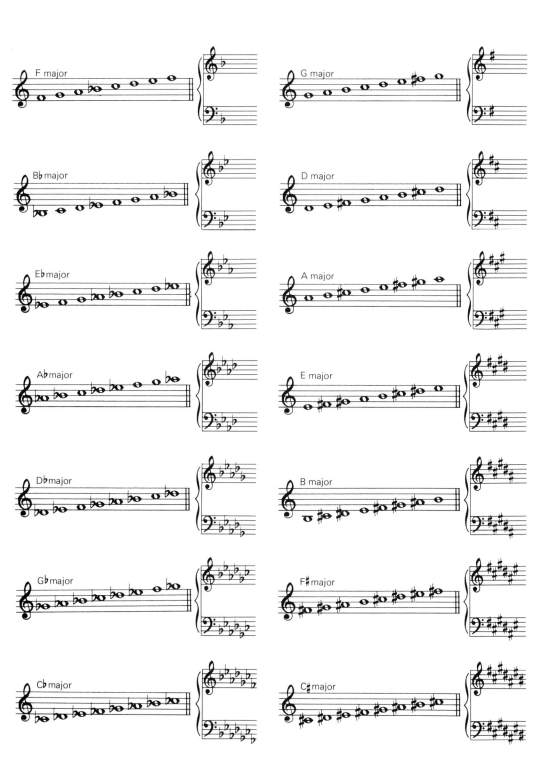

The key signature remains in effect in all octaves throughout a composition or until a change of key is indicated. Sharps or flats, as designated by the key signature, may be canceled by naturals, which are valid only for the measure in which they appear. For example:

CIRCLE OF FIFTHS

In addition to being pictured as in the diagram on page 80, the major scale and key system may be represented graphically as a **circle of fifths**. (A fifth is the pitch difference between the first and fifth notes of a scale.) Notice that at three points the circle overlaps, so that the keys Db and C♯ are enharmonic, as are Gb and F♯ and Cb and B.

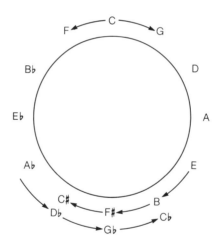

LEARNING AIDS

The above presentation of material is intended to illustrate the logic of, and conventions associated with, the major scale and major key system. For the practical musician, however, it is material that must be committed to memory.

Two learning aids that may be helpful are:

1. Given a key signature in sharps, the sharp farthest right is the seventh scale step and the keynote or tonic will be the

scale degree a half step above. For example, if a signature has three sharps the last sharp is G♯, and therefore the tonic will be the next degree, A, and the key A major.

2. Given a key signature in flats, the flat farthest right is the fourth scale step and by proceeding down to the first scale step the tonic will be found. For example, if a signature has five flats and the last flat is G♭, by descending four scale steps the tonic will be found to be D♭ and the key D♭ major. *Or*, in the case of multiple flats in a key signature, the next to last flat is the tonic.

7.1 Exercises: Identifying Key Signatures

With the learning aids as guides, write the tonic for each of the following key signatures and name the key.

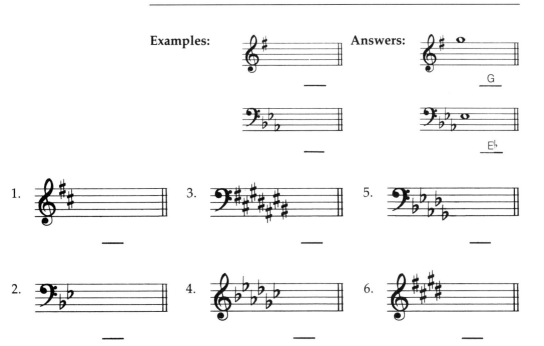

7.    9.    11.

8.   10.   12.

SCALE DEGREES

Each scale degree has a specific name. Each has a different relationship to the others, and each has its own characteristics.

Following are scale degrees and their characteristics, in ascending order.

Degree	Name	Characteristics
1	tonic	keynote; focal point and most stable tone; gives a sense of restfulness and finality
2	supertonic	above the tonic; unstable and active, with a tendency to move to tonic or mediant
3	mediant	midway between tonic and dominant; stable and restful; determines major or minor quality of scale
4	subdominant	the under-dominant; unstable and active, with a strong tendency to move to mediant
5	dominant	stable; focal point next in importance to tonic
6	submediant	midway between subdominant and upper tonic; unstable and active, with tendency to move to dominant
7	leading tone	most unstable and active, with strong tendency to move to tonic

HARMONIC SERIES

The relationships between and characteristics of the major scale degrees may be better understood with some knowledge of acoustics, the science that describes the physical basis of music.

As stated in Chapter 1 with regard to timbre, a tone consists of a basic pitch and a complex of higher pitches sounding sympathetically. Together they form a **harmonic series**. The basic pitch, the **fundamental**, is the loudest and is called the first **partial**. The other pitches are the second partial, third partial, and so on in order of diminishing strength in reinforcing the fundamental.

The first five partials of the harmonic series on C are:

Partials 2 and 4, both Cs, are octave reproductions of the fundamental and reinforce its predominance. The third and fifth partials, G and E, are the next closely related to C because of the strength of their sympathetic vibrations.

By representing the harmonic series within a one-octave range, as first, third, and fifth degrees of a major scale, their characteristics as stable pitches become evident.

𝗼 = stable, restful

● = unstable, active

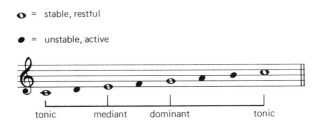

The other four scale degrees, far removed in strength from and proximity to the fundamental of the harmonic series, do not share the stability of the C, E, and G, and are therefore considered unstable and active in their tendency to move toward a point of repose.

In order to establish tonality in music, emphasis is given to the stable pitches—tonic, mediant, and dominant. The only pitches in evidence at the beginning of "The Star-Spangled Banner," for example, are F, D, and B♭, and these confirm B♭ as the tonal center or tonic.

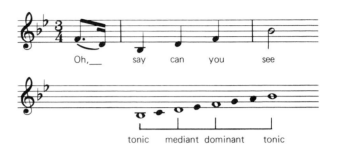

Although the beginning of "Joy to the World" consists of an entire descending D major scale, the pitches D, F♯, and A are emphasized through strong metric placement and long duration. The unstable pitches are on weak beats and are generally of shorter duration.

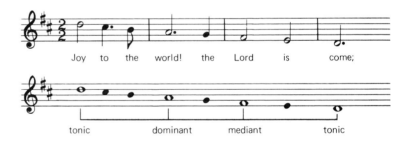

TRANS-POSITION

To **transpose** music is to move the tonal center while maintaining the corresponding scale steps of the original. Music is transposed to accommodate instruments or voices of different pitch ranges.

In transposing, the key is changed to establish a new tonic and the music is notated at a higher or lower pitch level. In the following examples, scale step numbers have been placed below the notes of the original. In the transposed version, a new key signature establishes a new tonic; scale step numbers remain the same. The melodic contour (upward and downward movement of pitch) of the original and that of the transposed version must be identical.

Original   **Transposed**

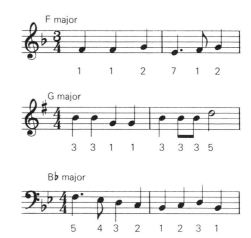

C major

scale steps   1   1   2   7   1   2

C major   F major

scale steps 3   3   1   1   3   3   3   5

C major   G major

D major   Bb major

scale steps   5   4   3   2   1   2   3   1

Note in the last example that transposition may involve a change of clef.

CHAPTER EXERCISES

1. Write the seven sharps in the order in which they appear in key signatures.

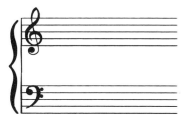

2. Write the seven flats in the order in which they appear in key signatures.

3. Using accidentals, add tetrachords to form major scales.

Example: above the given notes

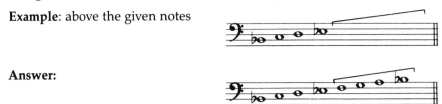

Answer:

a. above the given notes

b. below the given notes

4. Add sharps or flats to the following scales to form major scales. Then arrange the sharps or flats as key signatures.

Example:

Answer:

a.   b.

c.   d.

5. In half notes and with accidentals write the following scales. Then arrange the sharps and flats as key signatures.

   Example: B♭ ascending

   a. D major descending

   b. D♭ major descending

   c. F major ascending

   d. B major ascending

6. Write the following scale steps.

   Example: mediant in the key of D

   a. supertonic in the key of B♭
   b. subdominant in the key of F
   c. leading tone in the key of G
   d. dominant in the key of A♭

   e. mediant in the key of E
   f. submediant in the key of A
   g. mediant in the key of E♭
   h. dominant in the key of D

7. Transpose the following excerpts. First, write the new key signature followed by the meter signature. Then, write the scale step numbers under the staff. Finally, write the pitches, following the melodic contour of the original. (The first pitch of the transposed version is given.)

   a.
   5 1 1 1 3 2 1 7 6 5

   down to key of F

   5

b.

up to key of G

c.

down to key of D

d.

up to key of C (note clef change)

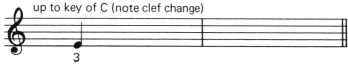

8. Below are beginnings of songs in which the tonality is established through emphasis on stable pitches. For each excerpt, determine which are the three stable pitches (scale steps 1, 3, and 5). Write the key signature. Then write in whole notes the stable pitches in the order in which they appear in the song. Above the staff indicate tonic (T), mediant (M), and dominant (D).

Example:

Oh, when the   saints_____   go march - ing   in,_____

Answer:

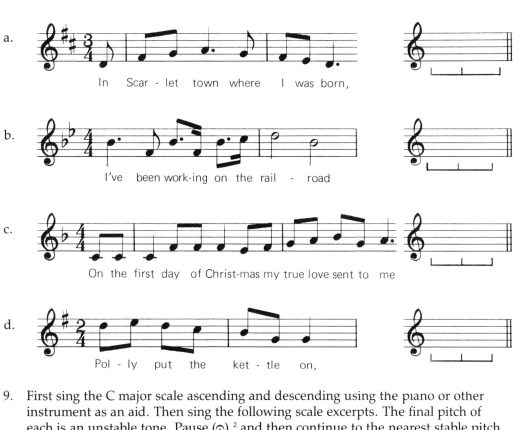

a. In Scar - let town where I was born,

b. I've been work-ing on the rail - road

c. On the first day of Christ-mas my true love sent to me

d. Pol - ly put the ket - tle on,

9. First sing the C major scale ascending and descending using the piano or other instrument as an aid. Then sing the following scale excerpts. The final pitch of each is an unstable tone. Pause (⌢),[2] and then continue to the nearest stable pitch. (In some cases there is a choice.) Write the pitch chosen.

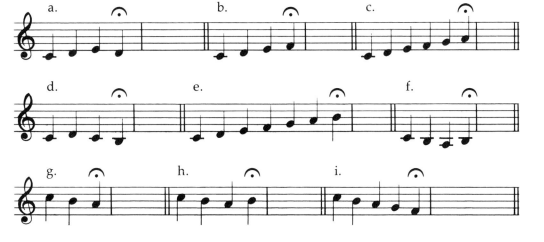

a.   b.   c.

d.   e.   f.

g.   h.   i.

---

2. *The Italian term for a pause or hold (⌢) is* **fermata**.

10. For each of the following examples play the tonic (middle C), and then at a moderate tempo sing the example using numbers, letter names, or syllables.

11. **Instructor**: Play various ascending and descending scales at the piano (major, minor, chromatic, modal). Have students identify those which are major.

PIANO EXERCISES

1. Play all of the major scales (pages 80–81) while looking at the notation.

2. Play the same scales descending while thinking of the major scale pattern of whole and half steps.

3. Play the illustrations of transposition (page 87). (Scale step numbers are not fingerings.)

4. Perform the melodic excerpts of Exercise 8 of the Chapter Exercises. After playing each excerpt, play and sustain the tonic, mediant, and dominant pitches.

Intervals

NUMERICAL INTERVALS

An **interval** is the distance in pitch, as measured in whole and half steps, between two tones. The ability to recognize intervals by sight and sound is essential in the study of music, as they are fundamental materials of melody and harmony.

If the two tones of an interval sound simultaneously and are represented vertically on the staff, the interval is a **harmonic interval**. If the two tones sound separately and occur one after the other on the staff, either ascending or descending, the interval is a **melodic interval**.

harmonic interval   melodic interval

All intervals are identified numerically, and the numerical name is determined by the number of lines and spaces encompassed by the interval. Ordinal numbers are used—*second, third, fourth, fifth, sixth, seventh*. Two tones on the same line or space are called a **prime**, and an **octave** spans eight lines and spaces.

Harmonic intervals above C are:

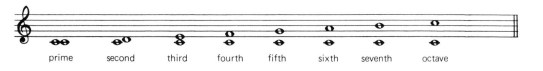

prime   second   third   fourth   fifth   sixth   seventh   octave

It is now possible to name numerically all intervals in music.

Humperdinck, *Hansel and Gretel*

8.1 Exercises: Numerical Intervals

---

1. Give the numerical name of each interval.

Example:

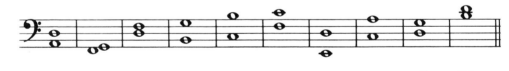

2. Write the specified numerical interval above the given note.

Example: **Answer:**

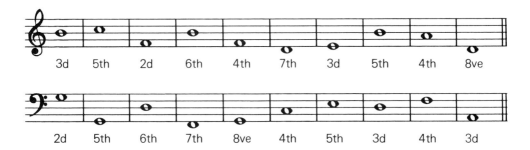

3d 5th 2d 6th 4th 7th 3d 5th 4th 8ve

2d 5th 6th 7th 8ve 4th 5th 3d 4th 3d

3. Write the specified numerical interval below the given note.

Example: **Answer:**

4th 4th

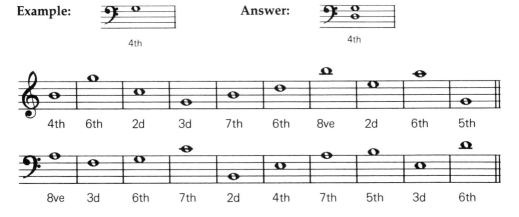

4th 6th 2d 3d 7th 6th 8ve 2d 6th 5th

8ve 3d 6th 7th 2d 4th 7th 5th 3d 6th

INTERVAL QUALITY

To classify an interval numerically the number of lines and spaces are counted. However, as can be seen in the example below, a third above G may be written several ways.

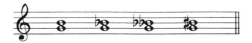

While the numerical name does not change, the sound does because each third has a different number of half steps. A *quality* designation is given to each of the thirds in order to distinguish one from the other. The qualitative terms, with the numerical intervals to which they apply, are given next.

- *perfect*   prime, fourth, fifth, octave

- *major* }
                     second, third, sixth, seventh
- *minor* }

- *augmented* }
                     any interval
- *diminished* }

Intervals may be understood in terms of a tonic and its relationship to other major scale steps. In the following illustrations C is tonic and the intervals are measured in whole and half steps.

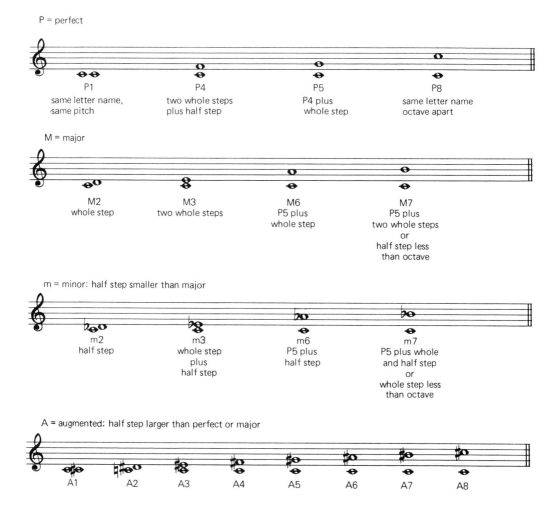

P = perfect

P1	P4	P5	P8
same letter name, same pitch	two whole steps plus half step	P4 plus whole step	same letter name octave apart

M = major

M2	M3	M6	M7
whole step	two whole steps	P5 plus whole step	P5 plus two whole steps or half step less than octave

m = minor: half step smaller than major

m2	m3	m6	m7
half step	whole step plus half step	P5 plus half step	P5 plus whole and half step or whole step less than octave

A = augmented: half step larger than perfect or major

A1   A2   A3   A4   A5   A6   A7   A8

d = diminished: half step smaller than perfect or minor

(there is no
diminished
prime)

d2   d3   d4   d5   d6   d7   d8

Many enharmonic equivalents are possible. In the following example the intervals are written differently but are identical in sound.

A4   d5

The quality classification of all intervals is shown in the following chart. The chart should be read starting from perfect and major . On either side are actual intervals exemplifying the quality designations of the chart.

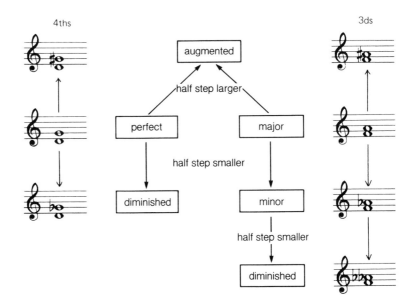

MAJOR AND MINOR SECONDS

With reference to the major scale, the half-step intervals between 3 and 4 and 7 and 8 may now be precisely designated as minor seconds. All other seconds in the major scale are whole steps or major.

scale steps   1   2   . 3   4   5   6   7   8

M2   M2   m2   M2   M2   M2   m2

Minor seconds are **diatonic half steps**, whereas half-step intervals between two notes with the same letter name are **chromatic half steps**.

diatonic   chromatic

COMPOUND INTERVALS

Intervals encompassing more than an octave are **compound intervals**. Ninths, tenths, elevenths, twelfths, and thirteenths are identified numerically as such. Their quality classifications are the same as those of their counterparts within the octave.

M9   (M2)   M10   (M3)   P11   (P4)   P12   (P5)   M13   (M6)

INVERSION OF INTERVALS

Inversion is a fundamental principle of music that offers melodic and harmonic variety while retaining original letter names. An interval is inverted if its lower tone is placed above the upper tone or vice versa. In the next example, the lower tone, C, is replaced by the upper octave C in the inversion.

P5   P4

The sum of the original interval and its inversion is always nine. Also, since an octave consists of twelve half steps, the number of half steps in the original interval plus the number of half steps in the inversion always equals twelve.

In the examples below, intervals are given with their inversions.

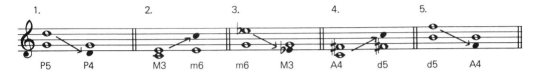

From the above examples the following conclusions may be drawn. When inverted:

1. A perfect interval remains a perfect interval.

2. Major becomes minor.

3. Minor becomes major.

4. Augmented becomes diminished.

5. Diminished becomes augmented.

ILLUSTRA-TIONS OF MELODIC INTERVALS

Following are excerpts from well-known songs with some melodic intervals identified.

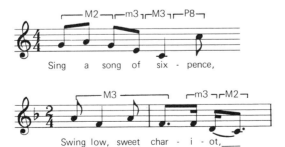

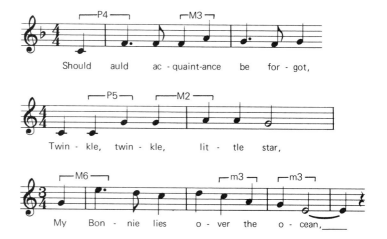

CHAPTER EXERCISES

1. Name the following intervals. Determine the numerical name first.

Example:

P5

___ ___ ___ ___ ___ ___ ___ ___

___ ___ ___ ___ ___ ___ ___ ___

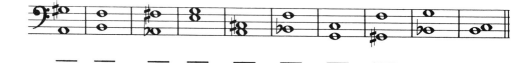

___ ___ ___ ___ ___ ___ ___ ___

2. Write a note above the given note to form the indicated harmonic interval.

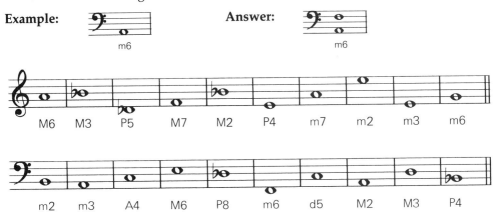

3. Write a note below the given note to form the indicated harmonic interval.

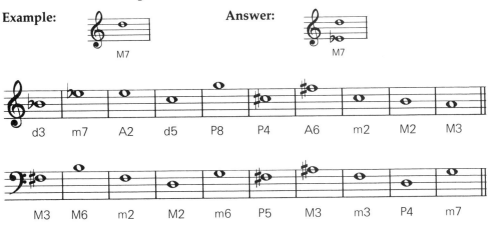

4. Name the following intervals. Then invert and rename.

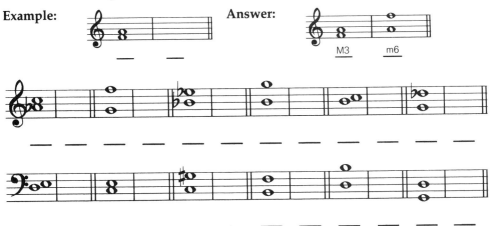

5. Identify all the melodic intervals in the following song.[1]

Note how tonality is established in the first measure with dominant moving to tonic and affirmed in the final two measures with scale steps leading from dominant to tonic. Note also the repetition of the initial two-measure rhythm pattern.

6. The following are ear exercises.

a. Sing from a tonic to each of the other scale degrees using numbers or syllables.

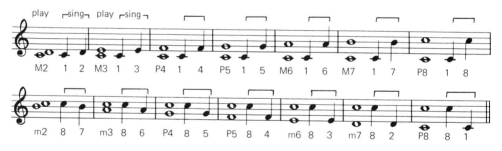

1. Similar in appearance to the tie, the **slur** is used to extend a syllable over two or more notes of different pitch.

b. At the keyboard, play the following intervals harmonically. Then sing the interval ascending and descending, using the keyboard to check accuracy.

Example:

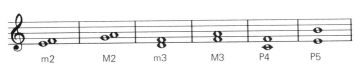

PIANO EXERCISES

1. Play both harmonically and melodically the illustrations of numerical intervals (page 93).

2. Play both harmonically and melodically the intervals in Exercise 8.1.1.

3. Perform the song excerpts illustrating melodic intervals (pages 99–100).

4. Play both harmonically and melodically the intervals in Exercise 1 of the Chapter Exercises.

5. Perform the song in Exercise 5 of the Chapter Exercises.

9

Compound Meter and Rhythm

COMPOUND METER

Meter is designated as **compound** if the beats are naturally divisible into three equal parts rather than two as in simple meter. As with simple meters, compound meters may be duple, triple, or quadruple, with the same patterns of accented and unaccented beats.

In compound meter the beat unit is represented by a dotted note, which divides into three.

- *beat*

- *division*

Each note of the division, however, divides naturally into two.

- *division*

- *subdivision*

The dotted half and dotted quarter most frequently serve as beat units in compound meter.

- *beat*

- *division*

- *subdivision*

COMPOUND METER SIGNATURES

In compound meter the beat unit is a dotted note, for which there is no corresponding number ($\quad$ = 4 but $\quad$ = ?). The lower number of the meter signature, therefore, indicates the note value of the *division*. The upper number gives the number of beat divisions in a measure.

Example: 6 ←——— six beat divisions per measure
8 ←——— beat division note value($\flat$)

Since the beat divisions per measure are in multiples of three—6, 9, or 12—the number of beats per measure is determined by dividing the upper number by three (6 = two beats, 9 = three beats, 12 = four beats). The resulting meters, then, are duple, triple, and quadruple, respectively.

Example: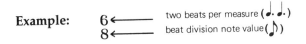

Although others are possible, the most frequently used duple, triple, and quadruple meter signatures are:

- *duple*

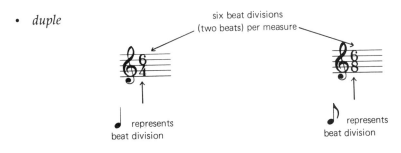

- *triple*

nine beat divisions
(three beats) per measure

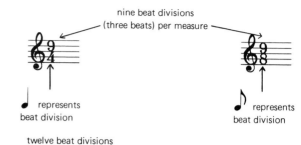

represents
beat division

represents
beat division

- *quadruple*   twelve beat divisions
(four beats) per measure

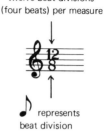

represents
beat division

9.1 Exercises: Compound Meter Signatures

---

1. Complete the following statements concerning the *upper* number of a compound meter signature.

   Example: Suppose the upper number of a compound meter signature is 6. This represents _two_ beats or _six_ beat divisions per measure.

   a. Suppose the upper number of a compound meter signature is 9. This represents _3_ beats or _9_ beat divisions per measure.

   b. Suppose the upper number of a compound meter signature is 12. This represents _4_ beats or _12_ beat divisions per measure.

2. Complete the following statements concerning the *lower* number of a compound meter signature.

   Example: If the lower number of a compound meter signature is a 2, the division note value is the _half_ note.

   a. If the lower number of a compound meter signature is a 4, the division note value is the _____ note.

   b. If the lower number of a compound meter signature is an 8, the division note value is the _____ note.

   c. If the lower number of a compound meter signature is a 16, the division note value is the _____ note.

3. Describe the following compound meter signatures.

Example: $\frac{9}{4}$ There are three beats per measure and the quarter note represents the division note value.

a. $\frac{12}{8}$ b. $\frac{6}{4}$ c. $\frac{9}{8}$ d. $\frac{6}{8}$ e. $\frac{9}{16}$

METERS AND RHYTHM UNITS

The most frequently used compound meters, together with the rhythm units (beats, divisions, and subdivisions) that constitute one measure, are:

- *compound duple meter*

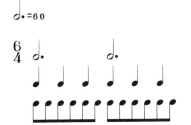

- *compound triple meter*

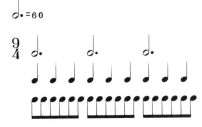
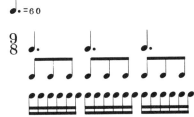

- *compound quadruple meter*

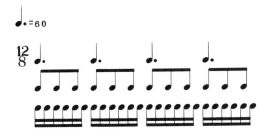

Of all compound meters, $\frac{6}{8}$ is most prevalent.

Notes are beamed so that the metric organization of each measure is clear.

Examples:

9.2 Exercises: Meters and Rhythm Units

1. With the class divided into two groups perform each of the duple, triple, and quadruple one-measure examples above as indicated.

   Group I taps a steady beat while intoning the beat numbers.

   Group II claps the division of the beat or intones rhythmic syllables.

   Repeat these one-measure patterns with characteristic metric accentuation until they can be performed with fluency.

2. For the excerpt below:

   a. Intone the words while conducting two beats per measure.
   b. Sing the words while tapping the beat.

$\bullet = 76$

f

Oh   dear,   what can   the   mat - ter   be ?   Oh   dear,

what can   the mat - ter   be?   Oh   dear,   what can   the   mat - ter   be?

John - ny's   so long   at   the   fair.

RHYTHM IN COMPOUND METER; COM-BINATIONS OF DIVISION

One-beat rhythm units resulting from combinations of division are:

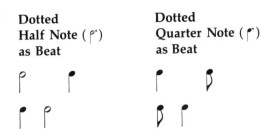

Dotted
Half Note (♩.) as Beat

Dotted
Quarter Note (♩) as Beat

9.3 Exercises: Combinations of Division

1. At a tempo of beat = 66, repeat each of the one-beat units above with a neutral syllable and pitch until the rhythm becomes familiar. Keep your eyes on the page so that the representation of the rhythm unit and its sound become integrated.

2. Below is an example of music in compound duple meter that includes combinations of division. Sing the words while tapping the beat or conducting.

RHYTHM; DIVISION AND SUBDIVISION COMBINED

One-beat units resulting from combinations of division and subdivision are:

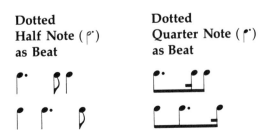

Dotted
Half Note (♩.) as Beat

Dotted
Quarter Note (♩) as Beat

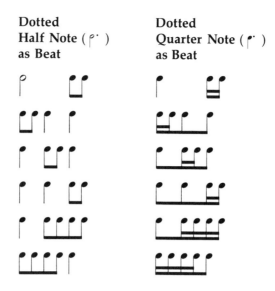

9.4 Exercises: Division and Subdivision Combined

1. At a tempo of beat = 60, repeat each of the one-beat units above with a neutral syllable and pitch until the rhythm becomes familiar. Keep your eyes on the page so that the representation of the rhythm unit and its sound become integrated.

2. Below are portions of familiar songs that include combinations of division and subdivision. Sing the excerpts while tapping the beat or conducting.

d.

He____ shall feed His flock like a shep - herd,

DURATIONS LONGER THAN THE BEAT

A duration longer than the beat is notated in one of the following ways.

- *by writing a single note value that combines beats*

- *by using ties*

Below are meters with a single duration that constitutes a full measure.

- *compound duple meter*

- *compound triple meter*

- *compound quadruple meter*

9.5 Exercises: Durations Longer than the Beat

1. With three groups, perform each of the following one-measure patterns at a moderate tempo, repeating until fluent.

   Group I sings the combinations of beat with beat division.

   Group II taps a steady beat while intoning beat numbers.

   Group III sings the combinations of beats.

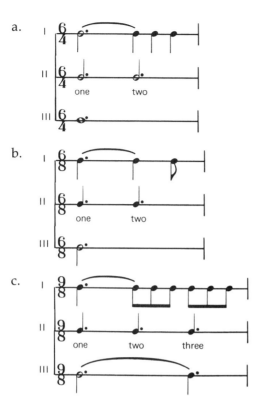

2. Below are portions of songs that include durations longer than the beat. Sing while tapping the beat or conducting.

a. ♩.=54 *p*

Down in the val - ley, the val-ley so low, Hang your head o - ver, hear the winds blow.

b. ♩.=40 *mf*

Home, home on the range,___ Where the deer and the an - te-lope play;_____

DUPLET

A **duplet** is a two-note group resulting from irregular division of a note that represents a compound beat. Duplets are recognized by a 2 written at the stem end of the group.

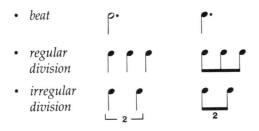

- beat
- regular division
- irregular division

Examples:

9.6 Exercises: Duplets in Compound Duple Meter

1. With two groups perform the above examples as follows.

   Group I taps a steady beat while intoning beat numbers.
   Group II sings on a neutral pitch and syllable.

   Repeat until fluent. Note that both examples sound identical.

2. Perform the following measures by tapping a steady beat while intoning the words. Note that the two syllables of "gar-den" have equal duration when spoken and are rendered musically with a duplet.

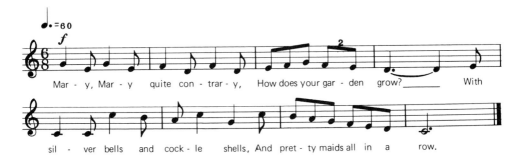

3. Find the pitches on the keyboard.

4. Sing the words in rhythm at the notated pitches, tempo, and dynamic level. Men may sing an octave lower.

TEMPO AND METER

As stated in Chapter 4, $\frac{3}{8}$ is a simple triple meter. At a fast tempo, ♪ = 300 or Prestissimo, a measure of $\frac{3}{8}$ assumes the feeling of a single compound beat, ♩. = 100. The following Christmas carol is fast enough to be felt in compound meter, one beat to the measure, rather than in simple meter, three beats to the measure.

At a slow tempo, ♪ = 100 or Largo, the compound meter $\frac{6}{8}$ has the feeling of six simple beats, $\frac{6}{8}$ ♩♩♩ ♩♩♩. "Sweet and Low," if performed slowly, is felt in simple meter, six beats to the measure, rather than in compound meter, two beats to the measure.

Where the tempo is very fast, as in "Bring a Torch, Jeannette, Isabella," a conductor may choose a conducting pattern that combines three simple beats. Beats 2 and 3 are included in the single upward gesture.

one to the measure

1

Where the tempo is very slow and it is difficult to feel a regular beat because the pulses are far apart, as in "Sweet and Low," a conductor may use a conducting pattern that reveals divisions as well as beats.

six to the measure

6

3 2 1 4 5

HEMIOLA

Hemiola is a type of syncopation in which the accents of syncopated notes result in a temporary shift in meter from simple to compound or vice versa. For example, in each of the following measures there is the same number of eighth notes but a different arrangement of beats and divisions.

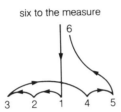

simple triple

compound duple

Hemiola results if music in compound meter shifts temporarily to simple meter through syncopation.

Example:

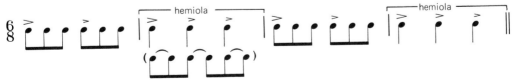

Hemiola also results if a compound pattern is superimposed on simple meter.

Example:

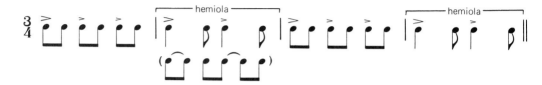

As a compositional device for creating rhythmic interest, hemiola has been used by composers from medieval times to the present. Below are examples.

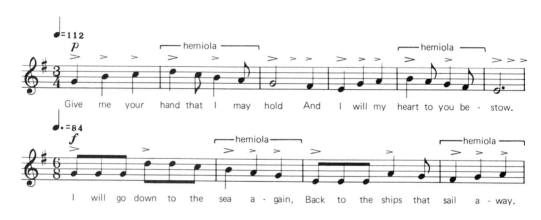

Give me your hand that I may hold And I will my heart to you be - stow.

I will go down to the sea a - gain, Back to the ships that sail a - way.

CHAPTER EXERCISES

1. Add bar lines to the following.

Example:

Answer:

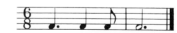

a.

2. Add meter signatures to the following.

Example: **Answer:**

d.

e.

f.

g.

3. Rewrite the following with, where appropriate, beams in place of flags.

Example:

a.

b.

4. Where a bracket occurs, add one note or two tied notes as an example of a duration longer than a beat.

Example:

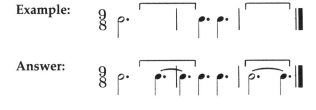

Answer:

a. $\frac{6}{8}$

b. $\frac{9}{8}$

c. $\frac{6}{4}$

5. Where a bracket occurs, add two or three notes as an example of beat division.

Example:

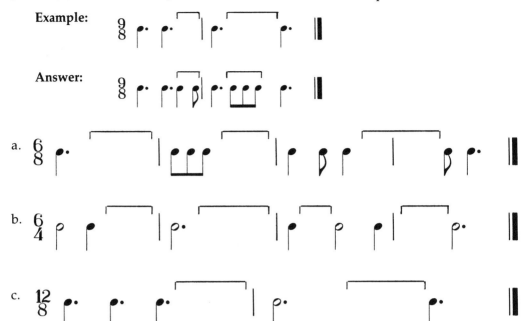

6. Where a bracket occurs, add notes illustrating combinations of beat division and subdivision. Use a variety of patterns.

Example:

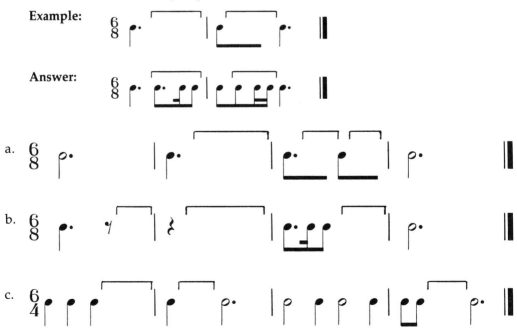

7. Where a bracket occurs, add a duplet.

Example:

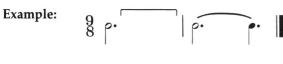

Answer:

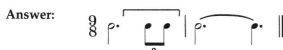

a.

b.

8. Complete the following by adding a measure illustrating hemiola.

Example:

Answer:

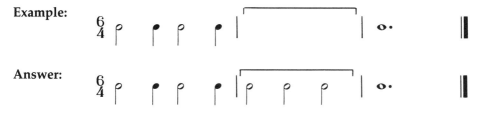

a.

b.

9. Below are rhythm patterns, one each in compound duple, compound triple, and compound quadruple meter. Add meter signatures and bar lines so that the metric emphasis of the notation and the emphasis of the words coincide.

Example:

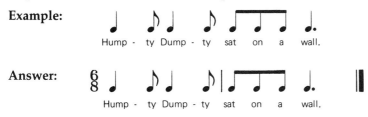

Hump - ty Dump - ty   sat   on   a   wall.

Answer:

Hump - ty Dump - ty   sat   on   a   wall.

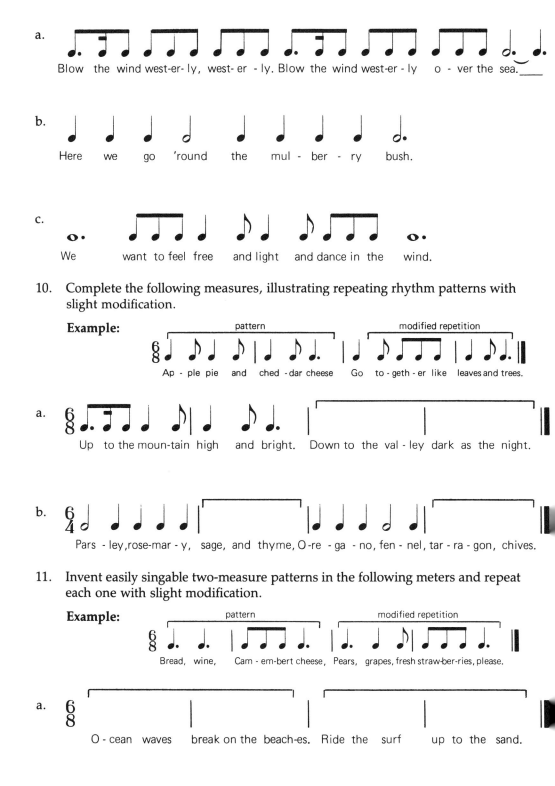

a. Blow the wind west-er-ly, west-er-ly. Blow the wind west-er-ly o-ver the sea.

b. Here we go 'round the mul-ber-ry bush.

c. We want to feel free and light and dance in the wind.

10. Complete the following measures, illustrating repeating rhythm patterns with slight modification.

Example:

pattern — modified repetition

Ap-ple pie and ched-dar cheese Go to-geth-er like leaves and trees.

a. Up to the moun-tain high and bright. Down to the val-ley dark as the night.

b. Pars-ley, rose-mar-y, sage, and thyme, O-re-ga-no, fen-nel, tar-ra-gon, chives.

11. Invent easily singable two-measure patterns in the following meters and repeat each one with slight modification.

Example:

pattern — modified repetition

Bread, wine, Cam-em-bert cheese, Pears, grapes, fresh straw-ber-ries, please.

a. O-cean waves break on the beach-es. Ride the surf up to the sand.

b.

Au-tumn is drea-ry, win - ter is sad.   Sum - mer is cheer-y, spring is glad.

12. Rewrite these rhythm patterns in the other meter indicated.

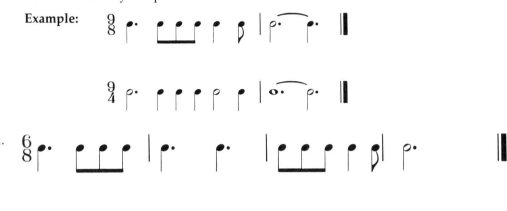

a.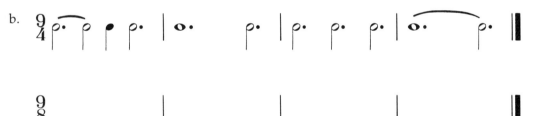

b.

c.

13. Find examples of repeating rhythm patterns in songs in compound meter.

14. Practice and be able to perform all of the exercises included in 1–10 above.

15. At a tempo of beat = 60, practice the following rhythm exercises until each can be performed fluently. Maintain a steady beat and use rhythmic syllables.

a.

b.

c.

d.

e.

f.

16. Rhythmic duets for additional practice.

Instructor: Begin by practicing each part separately. Sing as duets at an interval of a major third (or tenth).

a.

b.

PIANO EXERCISES

1. Using any pitch, play Exercise 15 of the Chapter Exercises.

2. With another person, each playing a different pitch, perform Exercise 16 of the Chapter Exercises.

3. Perform Exercise 9.3.2.

4. Perform Exercise 9.4.2(b).

5. Perform Exercise 9.5.2(a).

6. Perform the melodic excerpts under "Tempo and Meter" (page 114).

---

1. A **repeat** sign (at the double bars here) means repeat from the beginning or between signs 𝄆 𝄇 .

10

Minor Scales and Keys and Tonality

MINOR SCALES

As was seen in Chapter 7, there are *seven* seven-tone scales that begin on successive white keys of the piano keyboard, with the scale from C to C designated **major**. The scale on white keys from A to A is called **minor**. The scales of C major and A minor are **relative** major and minor; they share the same letter names and scale degree names (tonic, supertonic, and so on), but each has a different pattern of whole and half steps. The half steps in the minor scale are between 2 and 3 and 5 and 6.

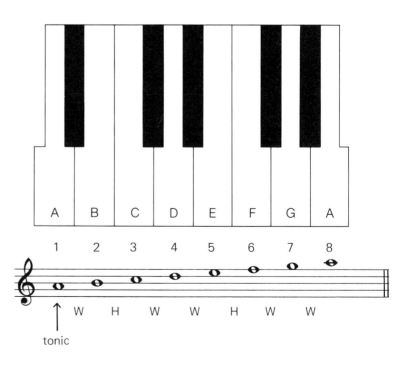

MINOR KEYS

There are major scales on all twelve pitches of the octave, and also twelve relative minor scales beginning an interval of a minor third below each major. Relative majors and minors share the same key signature.

G major   E minor

The order of major keys and their relative minors, the minors in lowercase letters, is:

C♭	G♭	D♭	A♭	E♭	B♭	F	C	G	D	A	E	B	F♯	C♯
a♭	e♭	b♭	f	c	g	d	a	e	b	f♯	c♯	g♯	d♯	a♯

← downward by perfect fifths   upward by perfect fifths →

Placed on the circle of fifths, the major and minor keys appear as follows.

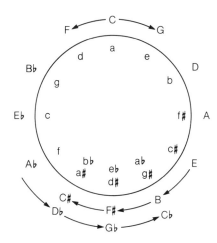

This represents the complete major-minor key system used in Western music.

All the minor scales and their key signatures are shown on the next page.

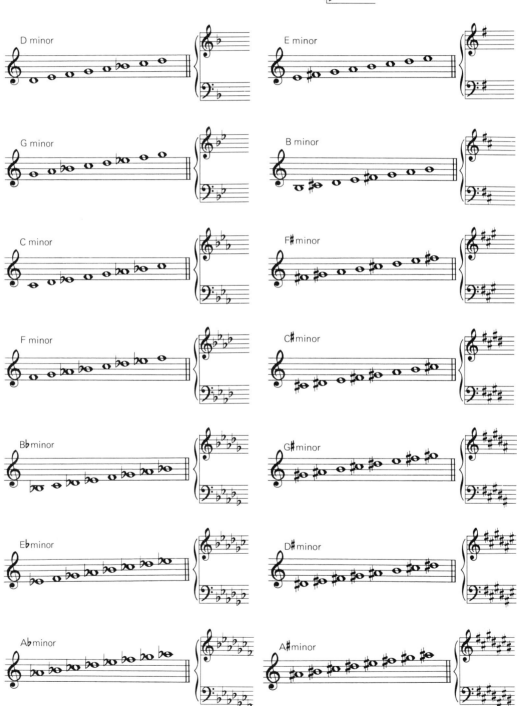

TONALITY, MAJOR OR MINOR

It is now evident that a key signature offers two possible tonalities for a musical composition. We know that tonality itself is fixed by the strength of the tonic and affirmed by the dominant. Therefore, although the two excerpts below share common key signatures, each has a different tonality owing to different tonics and dominants.

- *F major*

- *D minor*

PARALLEL MAJOR AND MINOR

While the tonic and dominant establish a basic tonality, it is the third scale step or mediant that imparts the characteristic sound of major or minor. The first five scale degrees of C major and C minor, for example, are different only because of the mediants, E and E♭, respectively. Major and minor scales that share the same tonic are known as **parallel** major and minor.

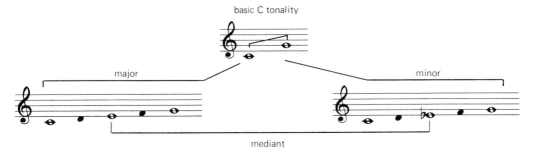

NATURAL, HARMONIC, AND MELODIC MINOR

Unlike the major scale, which has one pattern of whole and half steps, the minor scale may vary as a result of alterations in the upper tetrachord.

The **natural minor** or *pure minor* has the pattern of whole and half steps described at the beginning of this chapter, and is the same ascending and descending.

Example:[1]

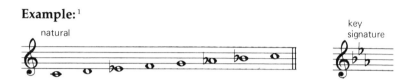

The **harmonic minor** employs a raised seventh step, giving the scale a leading tone that, through its activity both melodically and harmonically, strengthens the feeling of tonic. The seventh step maintains the same alteration descending.

Example:

The **melodic minor** borrows its upper tetrachord from the parallel major, and thus its sixth and seventh steps are raised. This gives the scale a leading tone but eliminates the augmented-second interval that appears between the sixth and seventh steps of the harmonic minor. Theoretically, the descending melodic minor reverts to the natural form of the scale; in practice, however, various forms of minor, ascending or descending, may be found in the same music.

---

1. *A seventh scale step a whole step from the tonic (B♭ in this example) is called the* **subtonic** *rather than the leading tone.*

Example:

melodic

key signature

Note that the key signature is the same for all three forms of the minor scale. Also, alterations of the sixth and seventh steps are made by means of accidentals in the music itself.

Here are four variations of the same melody. All have C as tonic. Because only dominant and tonic scale steps are present until the end of measure 1, all versions begin identically. In measure 2, where the sixth and seventh scale steps are used, each version is different. Measure 3, involving the lower part of the scale, varies only as to major or minor, depending on the mediant.

1. C major

I went to sea to see the world but all I saw was sea._____

2. C natural minor

I went to sea to see the world but all I saw was sea._____

3. C harmonic minor

I I went to sea to see the world but all I saw was sea._____

4. C melodic minor

I went to sea to see the world but all I saw was sea._____

Natural, Harmonic, and Melodic Minor   **131**

As with the major scale and key system, minor scales and key signatures must be committed to memory, and major-minor key relationships understood. Two learning aids that may be helpful are:

1. The tonic of a minor key is the interval of a minor third below that of its *relative* major; *or*, the sixth step of the major scale is the tonic of the relative minor, and, conversely, the third step of the minor scale is the tonic of the relative major.

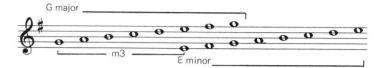

2. In *parallel* major and minor the minor scale has three steps, the third, sixth, and seventh, that are a half step lower than the same steps in major. These differences are reflected in the key signature.

CHAPTER EXERCISES

1. Below is a series of key signatures. Write the tonic of each major key and the tonic of its relative minor, and name both keys.

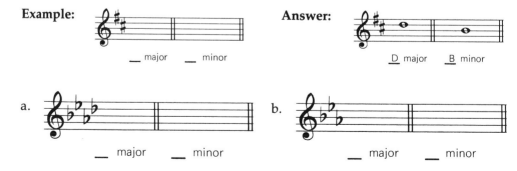

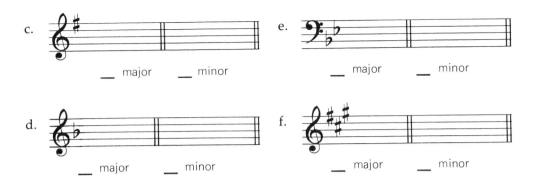

c. _____ major _____ minor

e. _____ major _____ minor

d. _____ major _____ minor

f. _____ major _____ minor

2. Below are major key signatures. Write the key signature of each parallel minor key and name both major and minor keys.

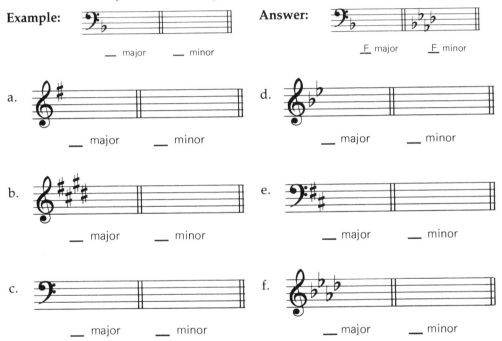

Example: _____ major _____ minor

Answer: _F_ major _F_ minor

a. _____ major _____ minor

d. _____ major _____ minor

b. _____ major _____ minor

e. _____ major _____ minor

c. _____ major _____ minor

f. _____ major _____ minor

3. Next are minor key signatures. Write the key signature of each parallel major and name both minor and major keys.

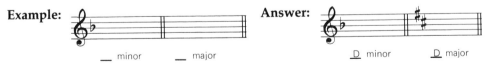

Example: _____ minor _____ major

Answer: _D_ minor _D_ major

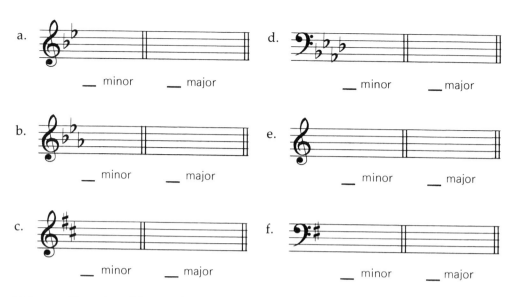

a. ___ minor ___ major

b. ___ minor ___ major

c. ___ minor ___ major

d. ___ minor ___ major

e. ___ minor ___ major

f. ___ minor ___ major

4. Using accidentals, add tetrachords to form the scales indicated.

Example: natural minor scale

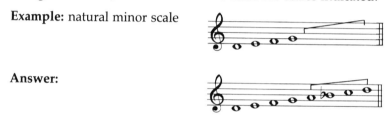

Answer:

a. natural minor scales

b. harmonic minor scales

c. melodic minor scales

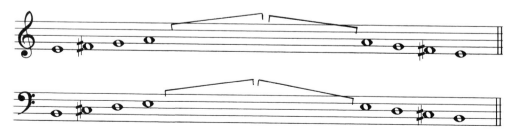

5. Add sharps or flats to the following scales to form natural minor scales. Then arrange the sharps or flats as key signatures.

Example: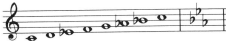

Answer: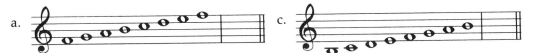

a. 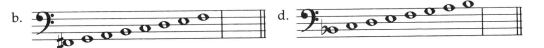   c.

b.   d.

6. In half notes and with accidentals write the following scales. Then write the key signatures.

Example: C harmonic minor descending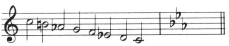

a. D natural minor descending

c. A harmonic minor ascending

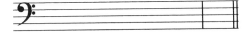

b. C melodic minor descending

d. G melodic minor ascending

7. Write the following scale steps.

Example: leading tone in the key of A minor

a. supertonic in the key of E minor
b. subdominant in the key of F minor
c. leading tone in the key of G minor
d. dominant in the key of F♯ minor
e. mediant in the key of B minor
f. submediant in the key of C minor
g. subtonic in the key of E minor
h. dominant in the key of D minor

8. Below are beginnings of songs in which tonality is established through emphasis on stable pitches. For each song write the key signature and the three stable pitches in the order in which they appear in the song, and above the staff indicate tonic (T), mediant (M), and dominant (D).

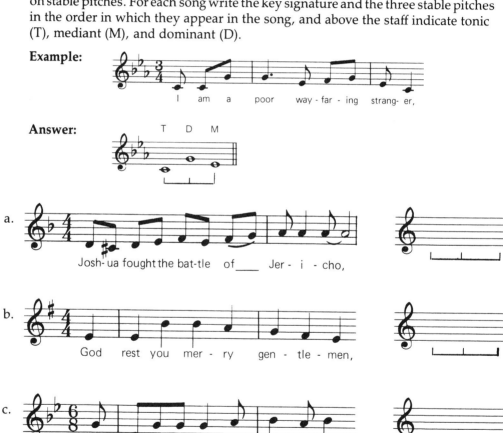

d.

We three kings of O - ri - ent are,

9. Transpose the following excerpts into the keys indicated. Begin by writing the new key signature.

a.

5 1 5 4 3 2 1 7 1

5

D minor

b.

1 5 1 3 2 1 5 6 7 1

1

C minor

c.

1 5 6 5 4 3 1

1

B minor

d.

1 7 6 5 6 7 1

1

A minor (note clef change)

10. First sing the three forms of the C minor scale ascending and descending using the piano or other instrument as an aid. Then sing the following C minor scale excerpts. The final pitch of each is an unstable tone. Pause (⌒) and then continue to a stable pitch. Write the pitch chosen.

11. For each of the following examples play the tonic (middle C), and then at a moderate tempo sing the example using numbers, letter names, or syllables.

e.

f.

g.　　　　　　　　　　　h.

12.　Be able to identify the three forms of the minor scale by ear.

PIANO EXERCISES

1.　Play all of the minor scales (pages 128–129), ascending and descending, while looking at the notation.

2.　Play natural, harmonic, and melodic minor scales ascending and descending on C, D, E, G, and A.

3.　Perform the melodic excerpts of Exercise 8 of the Chapter Exercises. After playing each excerpt, play and sustain the tonic, mediant, and dominant pitches.

A **melody** is a succession of individual pitches rhythmically impelled. **Form** is the process whereby the pitches and durations are organized into larger logical structures.

Each melody consists of some formal elements that give it *unity* (stability, rest, predictability, relaxation) and others that provide *diversity* (instability, activity, suspense, tension). A balance of unity and diversity creates interest in music.

MELODIC ORGANIZATION

Melodic organization, with "Silent Night" as an example, is examined below under the headings rhythm, pitch range, tonality, intervals, motives, phrases, period, and melodic contour and climax. Each brief analysis will reveal certain practices pertaining to melodic writing. After each analysis these practices will be restated as general principles of unity and diversity that apply to all melody.

Rhythm

Three metric units, ♩·, ♩♪, and ♩·♫, combine into five rhythm patterns, all interrelated.

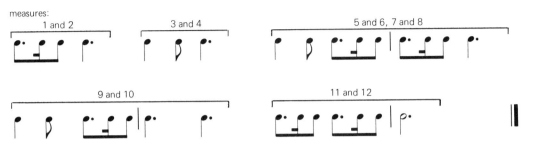

Recurring rhythm patterns maintain unity. Change or modification in rhythm patterns creates diversity.

Tonality

The tonality of C major is affirmed, through combinations of tonic, mediant, and dominant, in eight of the twelve measures. The C at the end gives final confirmation.

Tonality is a unifying factor. A change in tonality, infrequent in short melodies, offers diversity in music of larger scope.

Intervals

The first measure employs both motion by *step* (intervals of a second), ascending and descending, and motion by *skip* (intervals of a minor third or larger), descending.

Intervals of a second and third predominate in this melody, and their recurrence helps to maintain unity. The other intervals, minor seventh and perfect fourth, are used less frequently, and create diversity.

Motion by step is a unifying factor in a melody. Skips add diversity, the larger skips creating greater tension. Steps or skips moving upward generally tend to create more tension than those that descend.

Pitch Range

The pitch range is an octave and a fourth.

This is fairly wide, as most folk and popular melodies and carols encompass an octave to an octave and a third.

Melodies within a narrow range tend to be unified through stepwise motion, narrow intervals, and repetition, whereas melodies covering a wide range tend to be more diverse in intervallic structure.

Motives

A **motive** is the smallest meaningful melodic-rhythmic entity. The first motive in "Silent Night" consists of the material of the first measure.

Occurring again in measures 2, 6, and 8, it accounts for one-fourth of the melodic-rhythmic material of the carol.

Other motives, such as

and

are closely related to the first motive because of the similarity of their intervallic and rhythmic content.

The opening motive is usually the most important single element in providing unity because of its influence on subsequent material. Intervallic or rhythmic changes in the motive and the presentation of contrasting motives provide diversity.

Phrases

Motives combine into a **phrase**, the next largest meaningful group of musical ideas, comparable to a phrase in prose. A musical phrase is usually four measures in length. It ends with a **cadence pitch**, which is generally of longer duration than other pitches in the phrase, and provides temporary repose or a final conclusion. The degree of repose or finality depends on the stability or instability inherent in the scale step.

Unity in a phrase may be maintained by the use of *exact repetition* and *sequence*. In exact repetition a motive or melodic-rhythmic group is immediately repeated at the *same* pitch level, whereas in **sequence** it is immediately repeated at a *different* pitch level. The change of pitch level in sequence gives some diversity.

There are three phrases in "Silent Night," each of different construction.

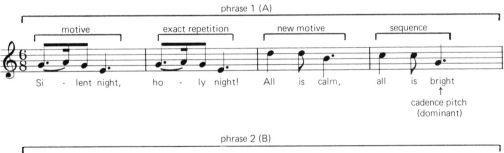

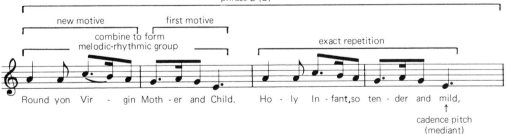

Phrase 1 (A) is the most balanced in unity and diversity because of the exact repetition of the first motive and because of the sequence of the second motive. Diversity is created by the leap of a seventh to the new motive in measure 3 and the change of interval in the sequence.

Phrase 2 (B) is the most unified because of the exact repetition and because only one new motive is presented.

Phrase 3 (C) has the most diversity as there are three new motives, there is no repetition, and the phrase encompasses the entire pitch range.

Period

A musical **period**, comparable to a sentence in prose, consists of two or three phrases that together form a complete musical idea. A two-phrase period is the most common. The end of a period is generally signaled by a cadence on the tonic, where a longer duration on the final note further enhances the feeling of finality.

"Silent Night" consists of a period formed by three contrasting phrases. The cadence pitches of phrases A and B are the dominant and mediant, which suggest repose. Phrase C has the tonic as cadence pitch; this pitch has the longest duration in the carol and thus the greatest feeling of repose and finality. The diversity of the phrase structure ABC is balanced by the unity maintained within phrases.

A **double period** consists of two consecutive periods. Some formal schemes for double periods are AABB ("Greensleeves"), AABA ("I Want to Hold Your Hand"), ABAB ("Down in the Valley"), and AABC ("Pop! Goes the Weasel").

Melodic Contour and Climax

A graphic illustration can be used to indicate pitch direction and reveal the focal point of a melody. This focal point or *climax* is often preceded by increasing tension and may be the highest or lowest pitch, the longest duration, or a combination of both. It is more likely to occur near the end of a melody.

Below is a graphic illustration, by phrase, of the melodic contour of "Silent Night."

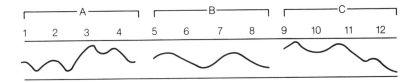

The contour confirms that the greatest pitch diversity occurs in phrase C. Other factors making the highest pitch of the phrase the climactic point of the carol are as follows.

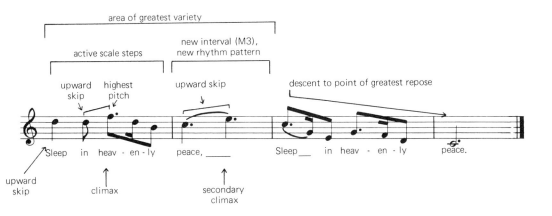

FURTHER ILLUSTRATIONS OF MELODIC ORGANIZATION

In "Greensleeves" unity is achieved by the repetition of rhythm pattern alone, as there is no motive repetition.

Rhythm

The first phrase of "All My Trials" has little rhythmic or melodic unity, but the second phrase balances this diversity with a new motive presented in sequence, the sequence ending on a tonic cadence pitch. The tension of the first phrase reflects the tension of the text. In the second phrase, relaxation is furthered by stepwise motion, a narrow pitch range, and sequence.

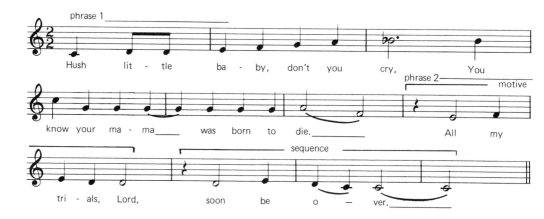

Tonality

"We Three Kings" is an unusual example of a change in tonality in a short composition. The change from minor to relative major is effected through the first measure of the chorus, which consists of active (unstable) pitches in both E minor and G major.

The active pitches and pauses combine to highlight the point of change and prepare for the new tonality. Stable pitches establish each tonality, which is then affirmed by its cadence pitch (tonic).

Motives

The beginning of "Lightly Row" has sequence.

The "Caisson Song" shows exact repetition and slight melodic and rhythmic modification.

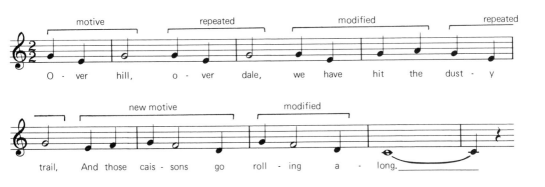

CHAPTER EXERCISES

1. Complete the missing portions of the following phrases. Be able to perform the completed phrases.

   Example:

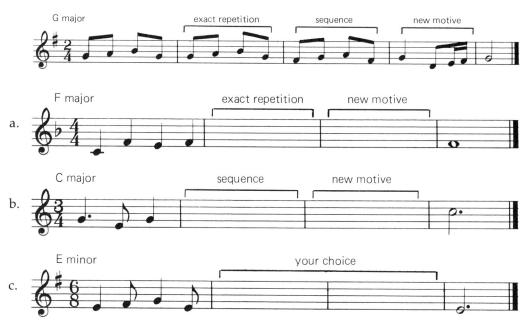

2. Provide cadence pitches for the following phrases. Be able to perform the completed phrases.

   Examples:

b. E♭ major   stable

c. C major   stable

d. G minor   unstable

3. Complete the following, providing the climax for each phrase. Be able to perform the completed phrases.

Example:

G major

F major

a.

C major

b.

A minor

c.

4. Study "All through the Night" and then answer the questions that follow.[1]

a. What is the tonic? _____ What is the key? _____
b. What is the pitch range? (Notate the lowest and highest notes.)

Is this a wide, narrow, or usual range for this type of music? _____
c. Notate the most prominent one-measure rhythm pattern. _____
d. Which is more prevalent, stepwise motion or skips? _____
e. What intervals other than major and minor seconds are used? _____
f. In the third phrase, put brackets over a one-measure motive (m) and its sequence (s).
g. The first two phrases form a _____. The entire melody comprises a _____. The formal scheme (use A, B, C, and so on) is _____.
h. Which phrase is most different from the others melodically? _____ rhythmically? _____

1. The measures in this and subsequent melodies are numbered beginning with the first complete measure.

i. Circle the cadence pitch of each phrase. Label as stable or unstable.

j. Place an arrow (↓) over the point of climax. Underline factors that make it the climax: highest pitch, long duration, area of greatest diversity, strong beat, active scale step.

5. Below are five melodies, each consisting of four phrases. Determine the following for each melody.

   a. the key

   b. the cadence pitch for each phrase and whether it is stable or unstable

   c. the formal scheme (use A, B, C, and so on)

   d. the pitch range

   e. the point of climax

"Deck the Halls"

"Aura Lee"

Au - ra Lee, Au - ra Lee, Maid of gold - en hair,

Sun - shine came a - long with thee, And swal - lows in the air.

"O Christmas Tree"

O, Christ - mas tree, O, Christ - mas tree, How com-fort-ing thy branch- es. O,

Christ- mas tree, O, Christ - mas tree, How com -fort-ing thy branch - es. They

are so green when sum-mer's here, And al - so green in win - ter drear. O,

Christ - mas tree, O, Christ - mas tree, How com - fort- ing thy branch - es.

"Early One Morning"

Ear - ly one morn - ing, just as the sun was ris - ing, I

heard a maid sing - ing in the val - ley be - low.

"Oh, nev - er leave ___ me, thy part - ing grieves_ me.

How__ could you use_____ a poor__ maid-en so?"

"Doxology"

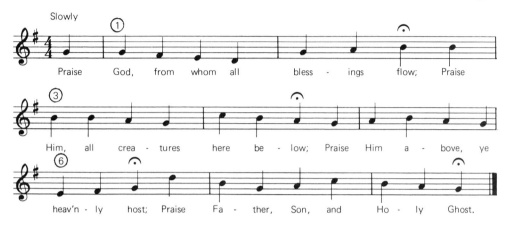

Slowly

① Praise God, from whom all bless - ings flow; Praise

③ Him, all crea - tures here be - low; Praise Him a - bove, ye

⑥ heav'n - ly host; Praise Fa - ther, Son, and Ho - ly Ghost.

6. Find the following.
   a. exact repetition of a one-measure motive in "Aura Lee"
   b. sequence of a two-measure melodic-rhythmic group in "O Christmas Tree"
   c. exact repetition of a two-measure melodic-rhythmic group in "Early One Morning"

PIANO EXERCISE

1. Perform "Deck the Halls," "Aura Lee," "O Christmas Tree," "Early One Morning," and "Doxology."

12

Harmony

Harmony is the simultaneous sounding of different pitches. It is the vertical structure of music, which complements the horizontal structure of melody.

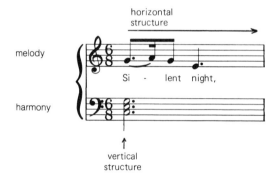

CHORD, TRIAD

The foundation of harmony is the **chord**, three or more pitches that appear in vertical alignment on the staff. In traditional Western music, chords are structured in intervals of a third above a tone designated as the **root**. Any scale tone may be the root, and a chord is identified by the scale tone that is its root— "tonic chord" and "dominant chord," for example. Below are three-tone chords, or **triads**, built on each scale step in C major.

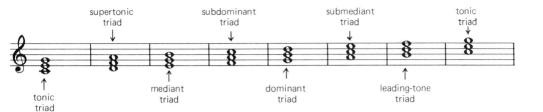

Triads in the position line-line-line or space-space-space are in **root position**. The notes above the root are the *third* and *fifth*, so named for their intervallic relationship to the root.

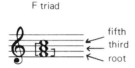

There are four types of triads, and the quality name of each is determined by its intervallic structure above the root. Their names, letter symbols, and intervals are:

• *major triad (M)*   major third and perfect fifth

• *minor triad (m)*   minor third and perfect fifth

• *diminished triad (d)*   minor third and diminished fifth

• *augmented triad (A)*   major third and augmented fifth

Triads may also be indicated by roman numerals. Uppercase numerals (I, IV, V) are used for major and augmented triads, lowercase numerals (ii, iii, vi) for minor and diminished triads. A + sign beside a numeral means augmented (III+), and a ° sign means diminished (vii°). The triads in C major indicated by roman numerals are:

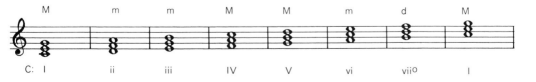

The triads in a minor key vary according to the form of minor scale used—natural, harmonic, or melodic. Those of the A harmonic minor scale, with roman numerals, are:

PRIMARY CHORDS

Just as there are relationships between scale degrees, so there are relationships between chords belonging to a key. The **primary chords** in a key are the tonic, dominant, and subdominant in order of their importance and frequency of use.

Chord Name	Description of Characteristics
• *tonic*	contains all stable tones and provides a harmonic center to which other chords are eventually drawn
• *dominant*	root a stable tone but third (leading tone) and fifth (supertonic) active tones
• *subdominant*	root (subdominant) and third (submediant) active tones but fifth (tonic) a stable tone

Secondary chords are the supertonic, mediant, submediant, and leading tone (or subtonic).

INVERSIONS OF CHORDS

A chord is **inverted** if a pitch other than the root is the lowest pitch. For example, an inverted triad has as its lowest pitch the third or fifth.

In a **first-inversion** chord the root is inverted and the third becomes the lowest note. In a **second-inversion** chord the root and third are inverted and the fifth becomes the lowest note.

Below is a root-position C major triad followed by its first inversion and second inversion.

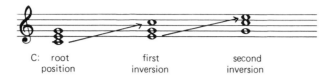

C: root   first   second
    position   inversion   inversion

No matter how the tones of a three-note chord are inverted or transposed by octave they are still designated a triad and the chord named for its root. All of the following are C major triads.

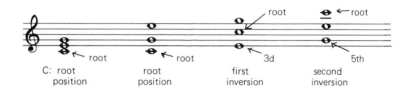

C: root   root   first   second
    position   position   inversion   inversion

To determine a chord root in music it is helpful to remember that the root is the lower note of the perfect fifth or the higher note of the perfect fourth, or their compound equivalents.

Inverted chords lack the stability of chords in root position, but do provide variety and a feeling of impending movement to a different chord.

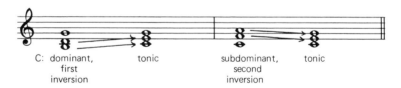

C: dominant,   tonic   subdominant,   tonic
    first   second
    inversion   inversion

DOMINANT SEVENTH

An interval of a third added to a root-position triad forms a four-note chord called a **seventh chord**. The seventh chord is named for the interval of a seventh between the root and the uppermost tone. The chord shown below is designated a *major-minor seventh* chord for the quality of the basic triad plus the quality of the interval of a seventh. The dominant seventh chord is represented symbolically as V7.

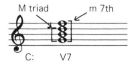

Although seventh chords of varying quality may be formed on any scale step, it is the major-minor seventh chord, or **dominant seventh**, that is found most consistently in tonal music. The added seventh, an active tone, gives the already active dominant chord additional impetus to move on to the tonic chord.

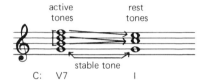

There are three inversions of the dominant seventh chord.

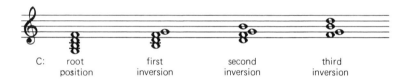

CHORD SYMBOLS

In folk music, popular music, and jazz, symbols written above the staff indicate chords. Capital letters designate chord roots and accompanying symbols specify chord quality. A capital letter alone stands for a major triad.[1]

---

1. *This system does not indicate whether the chord is in root position or inversion.*

MELODY AND ACCOMPANIMENT

Chord symbols suggest a harmonic framework within which an accompaniment may be improvised.

Following is a melody with chord symbols. One chord continues until a change of chord is indicated.

Here is the same melody with the chords represented by the chord symbols notated in root position on the bass clef. One chord per measure provides a sustained accompaniment.

The use of the second inversion of the subdominant chord and the first inversion of the dominant seventh chord allows smoother movement from chord to chord. Omitting the fifth from the V7 chord does not lessen the chord's effectiveness.[2]

Rhythmic activity is increased if portions of the chord are played on each beat.

---

2. *Directions for piano hand position and fingering are given in Appendix C, pages 204, 205.*

Rhythmic activity is further increased by a "broken chord" accompaniment. Although the chord tones do not sound simultaneously, the ear perceives them as harmonic units.[3]

MELODY AND HARMONY

If chord symbols for a melody are not designated, decisions must be made as to which chords are to be used and where they are to be placed.

The pitches of a melody imply chords with which to create an accompaniment. For example, in measure 1 of our melody pitches F and A imply the root and third of an F triad. Pitches such as these that are part of the harmony are called **chord tones**, and those that are not, such as the B♭, are **nonchord tones** or **nonharmonic tones**.

Chord tones are generally:

1. in strong metric positions

2. of longer durations

3. repeated in the same measure

In the next example, the first note of each measure will be a chord tone because it is in a strong metric position (all mea-

---

3. Note the slurs in this example. In instrumental music, the slur indicates that notes of different pitches are to be played smoothly.

sures), has longer duration (measures 2, 4, and 6–8), or is repeated (measures 4 and 7).

After these principal chord tones have been determined, accompanying chords may be chosen with the following points in mind.

1. The tonic chord appears at or near the beginning and at the conclusion of the melody.

2. Primary chords should be given priority.

3. Other pitches in the same measure combine with the principal chord tone to imply a single chord.

4. Chords usually change on strong beats.

The chords chosen to accompany our melody and the reasons for choosing them are as follows.

Measure	Chord Chosen	Reasons
1	F	1–4
2	F	2 and 3
3	B♭	2–4
4	F	Although the C7 chord is also implied, the F chord is the strongest primary chord, and provides more variety since the C7 follows in measure 5
5	C7	2–4
6	F	2–4
7	C7	Of the primary chords, it is the only possible choice
8	F	1, 2, and 4

Nonchord or **nonharmonic tones** are not part of the harmony. They add interest and variety, and are a means of moving smoothly from one chord tone to another in a melodic line. Two of the most common types are **passing tones** and **neighbor tones**. A passing tone (PT) connects by step two different chord tones. A neighbor tone (NT) connects by step two chord tones of the same pitch.

Nonchord tones are labeled in the example below.

Nonchord tones are generally:

1.   in weak metric positions

2.   of short duration

CADENCE

A **cadence** is a melodic-harmonic pattern occurring at the end of a phrase.

Harmonic cadences are specific chord patterns determined by the melody. Some are conclusive or **terminal**, others are inconclusive or **progressive**. The last phrase of a piece ends with a terminal cadence.

Progressive cadences represent instability and imply continuation because they usually end on the dominant chord. Two examples of progressive cadences are:

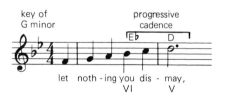

Terminal cadences represent the greatest degree of finality because they end on the tonic chord. Any phrase may end with a terminal cadence. Two examples of terminal cadences are:

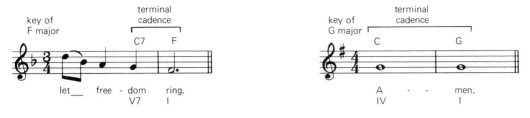

Progressive and terminal cadences are shown in the following two-phrase excerpts.

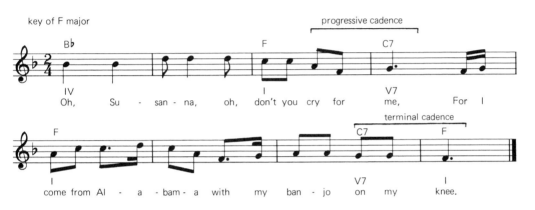

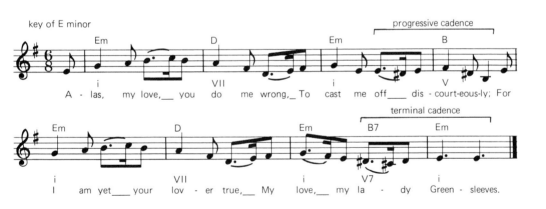

CHAPTER EXERCISES

1. Write the following root-position chords in the keys given. Place identifying roman numerals below the staff.

    Example: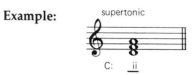

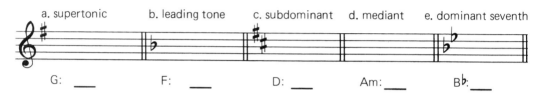

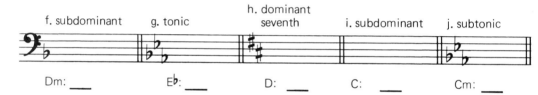

2. Add accidentals to the following chords so that they conform to the type indicated. Leave the chord roots as written.

    Example: **Answer:**

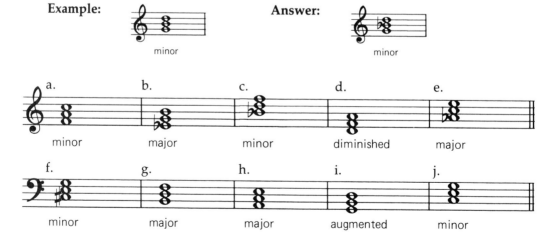

3. Write the primary triads in root position in the following keys. Use the harmonic form for minor keys (that is, raise the seventh scale step).

Example:

key of G minor

i   iv   V

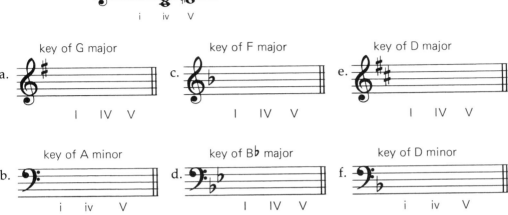

key of G major

a.   I   IV   V

key of F major

c.   I   IV   V

key of D major

e.   I   IV   V

key of A minor

b.   i   iv   V

key of B♭ major

d.   I   IV   V

key of D minor

f.   i   iv   V

4. Invert the following chords.

Example:

root   1st   2d

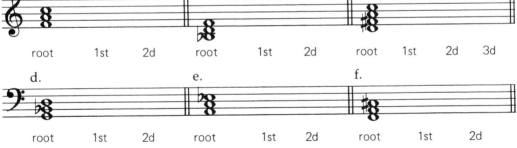

a.
root   1st   2d

b.
root   1st   2d

c.
root   1st   2d   3d

d.
root   1st   2d

e.
root   1st   2d

f.
root   1st   2d

5. Circle the roots of the given chords.

Example:

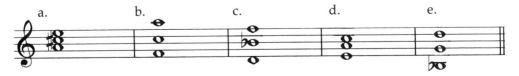

a.   b.   c.   d.   e.

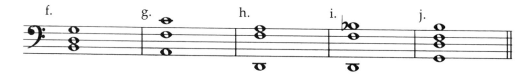

6. Under the staff write roman numerals that correspond to the chord symbols given. Identify cadence types. Circle and identify nonchord tones.

7. Above the staff write chord symbols that correspond to the roman numerals given. Identify cadence types.

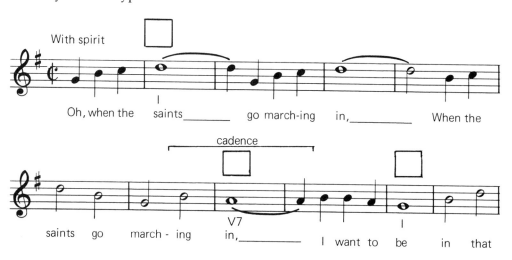

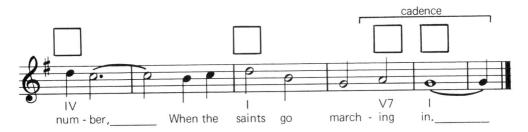

IV
num - ber,_____   When the   saints   go   march - ing   in._____

I   V7   I

8. Assuming one chord per measure, decide which notes should be chord tones. Choose appropriate chords from I, IV, V, and V7. Write roman numerals below the staff and chord symbols above the staff. Be able to identify nonchord tones and cadences.

PIANO EXERCISES

1. Play all chord types presented in this chapter and listen to the quality of each chord.

2. Refer to Appendix C, "Chords." With the left hand practice the primary chord pattern I, IV, V7, I in C major, F major, G major, and D major, and i, iv, V7, i in A minor, E minor, D minor, and C minor. Accompanying chords sound best in the octave below middle C.

3. From "Melody and Accompaniment" (page 159) perform the third musical example.

4. Perform the melody of Exercise 7 of the Chapter Exercises with accompanying chords.

13

Writing a Song

This chapter deals with the actual writing of a piece of music. Previous chapters have provided the fundamentals concerning pitch and rhythm, key and tonality, elements of good melody, metric accentuation of words, and harmony. The knowledge and skills gained will now be applied to the creation of a two-phrase melody for a verse of poetry.

STEP-BY-STEP PROCEDURE

One method for setting a verse of poetry to music is demonstrated in the step-by-step example below. Then, in the Chapter Exercise, another verse of poetry is given and the step-by-step procedure is to be followed by the student. As options, an accompaniment may be created for the resulting song and extra verses of poetry included at the end of the exercise may be used for further practice.

The poetry for the example is from Percy Bysshe Shelley's "Lines: 'When the Lamp Is Shattered.'"

When the lamp is shattered

The light in the dust lies dead—

When the cloud is scattered

The rainbow's glory is shed.

1. Recite the poem and mark the stressed syllables.

   When the lamp is shattered

   The light in the dust lies dead—

   When the cloud is scattered

   The rainbow's glory is shed.

2. Choose the meter. Arrange the words into two four-measure phrases, allowing a longer duration for a cadential syllable. Invent and notate the rhythm, making strong beats coincide with stressed syllables. If possible, unify the phrases with some rhythmic repetition. Check to ensure that durations in each measure conform to the meter.[1]

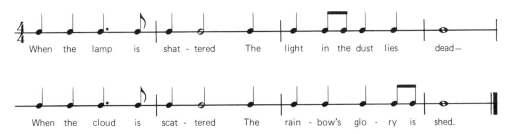

3. Choose a key and invent a chord pattern for each phrase. Write the chord tones on the staff in whole notes with chord symbols above and roman numerals below. These will serve as a guide in choosing melodic pitches for step 4.

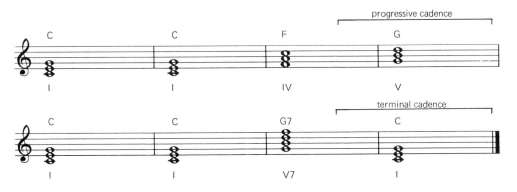

---

1. *Note in the example that words of more than one syllable are hyphenated and each syllable is represented by at least one note.*

4. Add pitch to the rhythm pattern of step 2 by choosing pitches for strong beats from the above chords and connecting some of the pitches with nonchord tones on weak beats or weak parts of beats.

5. Rewrite the completed melody. Add chord symbols from step 3 above the staff at the points where the first chord is introduced and where chord changes occur. Add dynamic markings and, above the meter signature, indicate the tempo.

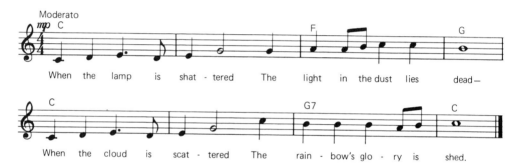

The "lead sheet" from which performers may read the melody and improvise an accompaniment is now complete.

CHAPTER EXERCISE

Set this poem by Christina Rossetti to music following the step-by-step procedure.

Boats sail on the rivers,

   And ships sail on the seas;

But clouds that sail across the sky

   Are prettier far than these.

1. Recite the poem and mark the stressed syllables.

> Boats sail on the rivers,
>
> And ships sail on the seas;
>
> But clouds that sail across the sky
>
> Are prettier far than these.

2. Speak the words while making conducting motions until a meter suggests itself ($\frac{3}{4}$, $\frac{4}{4}$, and $\frac{6}{8}$ are possibilities). Write the meter signature at the beginning of the first line. Arrange the words into two four-measure phrases by adding bar lines. Allow a longer duration for a cadential syllable. Invent and notate the rhythm, making strong beats coincide with stressed syllables. It is likely that the words "And," "But," and "Are" will appear on weak beats. If possible, unify the phrases with some rhythmic repetition. Check to ensure that durations in each measure conform to the meter.

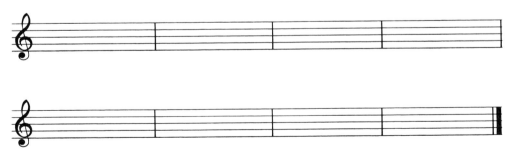

Boats   sail   on   the   riv - ers,   And   ships   sail   on   the   seas;   But

clouds   that   sail   a - cross   the   sky   Are   pret - ti - er   far   than   these.

3. Choose a key from C, F, and G major and invent a chord pattern (one chord per measure) for each phrase using only primary triads and the dominant seventh chord. Establish tonality at the beginning with a tonic chord. The first four-measure phrase may end with a terminal or progressive cadence. The second phrase must end with a terminal cadence. Write the chord tones on the staff in whole notes with chord symbols above and roman numerals below. Step 3 will serve as a guide in choosing melodic pitches for step 4.

4. Keeping the melodic principles of Chapter 11 in mind, add pitch to the rhythm pattern of step 2 by choosing pitches for strong beats from the chords chosen in step 3 and connecting some of the pitches with nonchord tones on weak beats or weak parts of beats. Write the notes directly above the syllables they set.[2]

Boats   sail   on   the   riv - ers,   And   ships   sail   on   the   seas;   But

clouds   that   sail   a - cross   the   sky   Are   pret - ti - er   far   than   these.

5. Rewrite the completed melody. Add chord symbols from step 3 above the staff at the points where the first chord is introduced and where chord changes occur. Add dynamic markings and, above the meter signature, indicate the tempo.

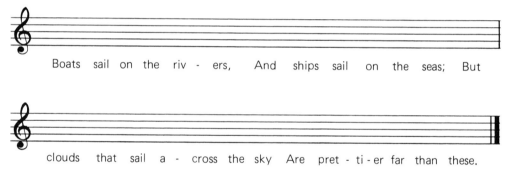

Boats   sail   on   the   riv - ers,   And   ships   sail   on   the   seas;   But

clouds   that   sail   a - cross   the   sky   Are   pret - ti - er   far   than   these.

6. (Optional) On music paper and using a grand staff, write the melody on the upper staff and invent an accompaniment on the lower staff. Accompaniments from Chapter 12 may be used as examples.

The poems on the facing page may also be set to music.

2. *Write the key signature after the first clef sign, and then the meter signature. On each staff after the first, repeat only the clef sign and key signature.*

The ostrich is a silly bird,

With scarcely any mind.

He often runs so very fast,

He leaves himself behind.

Mary E. Wilkins Freeman

Give a man a pipe he can smoke,

Give a man a book he can read;

And his home is bright with a calm delight,

Though the room be poor indeed.

James Thomson

I asked my mother for fifty cents

To see the elephant jump the fence,

He jumped so high that he touched the sky

And never came back till the Fourth of July.

Anonymous

PIANO EXERCISES

1. Perform the melody and accompanying chords in step 5 of the song-writing example (page 170).

2. Perform the melody and accompanying chords of step 5 of the Chapter Exercise when it has been completed.

14

Other Melodic, Harmonic, and Rhythmic Concepts

OTHER SCALES

Seven-Tone Scales

There are diatonic seven-tone scales other than major and minor. Known as **modes**, they were in evidence for many centuries before the development of the major-minor tonal system and have coexisted with major and minor to the present time. Modes may be represented beginning on the white keys of the keyboard.

The seven modes are:

1. *Ionian* mode, identical in pattern to the major scale.

2. *Dorian* mode, similar to the natural minor scale except that the sixth step is a half step higher.

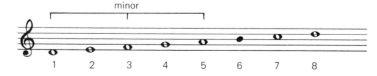

3. *Phrygian* mode, similar to the natural minor scale except that the second step is a half step lower.

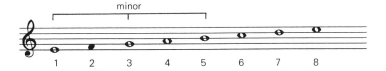

4. *Lydian* mode, similar to the major scale except that the fourth step is a half step higher.

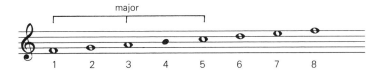

5. *Mixolydian* mode, similar to the major scale except that the seventh step is a half step lower.

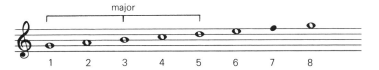

6. *Aeolian* mode, identical in pattern to the natural minor scale.

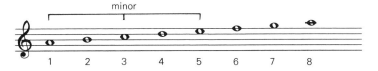

7. *Locrian* mode, not definitive in tonality since the interval between the first and fifth steps is a diminished fifth; rarely used.

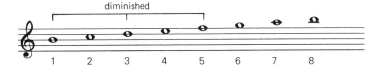

The example below is in the Dorian mode.

What shall we do with a drunk-en sail - or, What shall we do with a drunk-en sail - or,

What shall we do with a drunk-en sail - or, Ear - ly in the morn - ing?

As with major and minor scales, modes may be transposed to other pitch levels. This example is in the Mixolydian mode on D.

He used to live on a moun-tain top But now he lives in town. He

hangs his hat at the big ho - tel, Court - ing Bet - sy Brown.

Six-Tone Scales

Six-tone, or **hexatonic**, scales are also possible. Arranged in order, a series of six whole steps is known as the **whole-tone scale**, which has had limited use for the past century. The tonality of this scale is not clearly defined, because of the absence of a perfect fifth.

augmented

1 2 3 4 5 6 (1)

It is unlikely that the whole-tone scale would be the basis for an entire composition, but, as with the chromatic scale, portions are often used for coloristic or expressive effect. Below, the whole-tone scale is used only in the first four measures of the melody.

Moderato

Am   E+   A   C+   F

Whis - per - ing   leaves   are   say - ing   that   fall   is   nigh._____

Five-Tone Scales

A five-tone, or **pentatonic**, scale consists of five tones to the octave and includes two intervals of a third. One such scale may be illustrated by playing the black keys of the piano. The scale assumes a different character depending on its arrangement; for example, the first of the scales below has a major sound and the second a minor sound.

major   minor

1 2 3 4 5 (1)   1 2 3 4 5 (1)

The pentatonic scale above, characterized by the absence of half steps, is found in the music of many other cultures, including the music of China and Africa. The "Skye Boat Song" is Scottish in origin, and is based on a pentatonic scale of the major type but transposed to G and encompassing the notes G, A, B, D, and E.

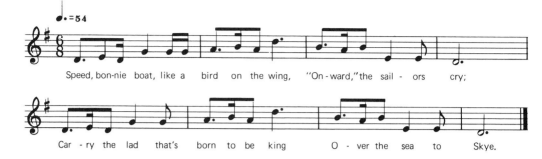

Speed, bon-nie boat, like a bird on the wing, "On-ward," the sail - ors cry;

Car - ry the lad that's born to be king O - ver the sea to Skye.

Pentatonic scales with half steps are prevalent in Asian music. Three illustrations are given below. The tuning of these scales as played on Asian instruments would vary slightly from Western tuning.

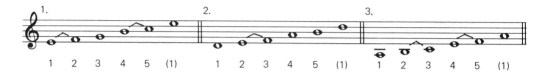

An example of the third type of pentatonic scale is found in the Japanese folk song "Sakura."

Sa - ku - ra, Sa - ku - ra, Ya - yo - i - no so - ra - wa, Mi - wa - ta - su ka - gi - ri.

Blues Scale

The seven-, six-, and five-tone scales by no means exhaust scale possibilities. Any number of other scales are feasible depending on the arbitrary selection of scale tones. The **blues scale**, for example, has several variations, the most prevalent being that of the major scale with the addition of "blue" notes.

Following is "Lonely Bird Blues" using the above scale. It is in the formal twelve-bar blues structure of three phrases, each four measures in length. The chord pattern is also basic.

"Lone - ly Bird Blues,"_____ I'm sing - in' them by my - self._____

"Lone - ly Bird Blues,"_____ I'm sing - in' them by my - self._____

Got - ta blame a wo - man_____ for put - tin' me on the shelf._____

OTHER CHORDS

Seventh Chords

Chords other than the dominant may have a seventh added. The seventh chords on the steps of the C major scale are given below, the chord name indicating both the quality of the basic triad and the quality of the interval of a seventh above the root. Four types of seventh chords emerge—the *major seventh, minor seventh, major-minor seventh,* and *half-diminished seventh.*

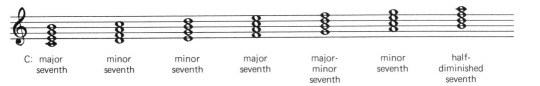

C: major seventh   minor seventh   minor seventh   major seventh   major-minor seventh   minor seventh   half-diminished seventh

The seventh chords on steps of the harmonic minor scale create three more seventh-chord possibilities—*minor-major seventh, augmented-major seventh,* and *diminished seventh.*

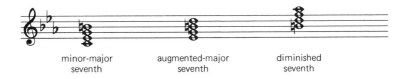

minor-major seventh   augmented-major seventh   diminished seventh

Here is a portion of "Twinkle, Twinkle, Little Star" accompanied by all of the seventh chords of a major key, moving in parallel motion.

Ninth, Eleventh, and Thirteenth Chords

Intervals of a third may be added above a seventh chord to produce **ninth**, **eleventh**, and **thirteenth chords**. Most are extensions of the dominant seventh and add color and tension to it. Alterations may be made above the seventh for variety. Some examples are:

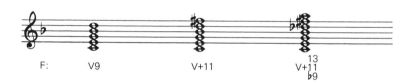

Nontertian Chords

Seventh, ninth, eleventh, and thirteenth chords are all **tertian**, or built in intervals of a third. In twentieth-century music, chords are often constructed of other intervals. Intervals of a fourth result in **quartal chords**, intervals of a fifth in **quintal chords**, and intervals of a second in **cluster chords**.

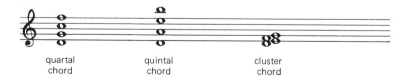

Next is a phrase of "Twinkle, Twinkle, Little Star" accompanied by quartal chords.

Added Tones

Tones are often added to nondominant chords; such tones are called **added tones**. For example, the major sixth or major ninth, or both, may be added to the tonic chord without altering its function as a point of repose.

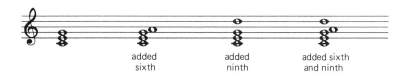

added
sixth

added
ninth

added sixth
and ninth

In both added-tone chords and extended-dominant chords, root positions are advisable for clarity and solidity.

OTHER METERS

Asymmetrical Meters

Some music, particularly that written in this century, stimulates interest and rhythmic propulsion through the use of **asymmetrical meters**. An asymmetrical meter may combine beats into groups of two and three. In *simple quintuple meter*, or $\frac{5}{4}$, the quarter note is the beat unit and each beat is of the same duration. The beats, however, combine in either of two ways:

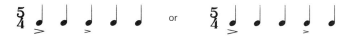

Here is a melody as it is usually notated.

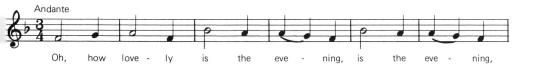

Oh, how love - ly is the eve - ning, is the eve - ning,

Tap the beats and sing the same melody as adapted to the asymmetrical pattern of three plus two beats.

Asymmetrical meters also combine simple and compound beats, as in $\frac{5}{8}$, $\frac{7}{8}$, and $\frac{8}{8}$ meters. Here the beats are not all of the same duration but the division unit (♪) is constant.

- *duple*

- *triple*

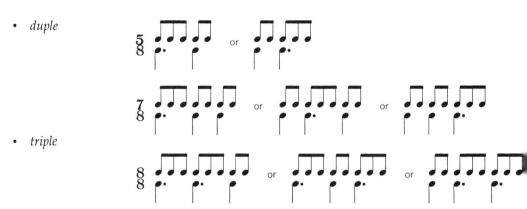

Below is an example of an asymmetrical measure division of three plus three plus two (♩. + ♩. + ♩).

Mixed Meters

In some music **mixed meters** occur, so that although beats may have the same duration, fixed patterns of strong and weak beats do not recur throughout. Similar patterns do not recur in "Shenandoah," for example, where various simple meters alternate.

Oh, Shen - an - doah, I long to hear you,___ A - way, you roll - ing

riv - er. Oh, Shen - an - doah, I long to hear you,___ A - way, I'm bound a -

way, 'Cross the wide Mis - sou - ri.____

When simple and compound meters are mixed, the relationships of beats in both meters must be indicated as follows: ♩· = ♩ or ♪ = ♪. For example, here one beat in $\frac{6}{8}$ time has the same duration as one beat in $\frac{2}{4}$ time.

But here the beat division has the constant duration and the beats are therefore of unequal length.

Mixed meters may also include symmetrical and asymmetrical meters in the same music.

The beat itself may be divided asymmetrically into five, seven, and so on. It is then identified by a number, similar to the 3 denoting a triplet, to show the division or subdivision.

CHAPTER EXERCISES

1. Identify the scales that the following melodies utilize. Write out each scale and then name it. Tonics are given.

d.

scale name:_____

e.

scale name:_____

2. Play all the chord types introduced in this chapter on the piano, listening to the quality of each. Sing each pitch moving upward from the root.

3. Make the following triads into major-minor seventh chords (that is, dominant sevenths) by adding a third above.

4. By adding a third above, make the following triads into the quality of seventh chord signified.

major
seventh

minor
seventh

half-
diminished
seventh

diminished
seventh

5. Match the chord quality types listed below to the chords illustrated by writing the appropriate letters in the blanks.

   a. quartal
   b. minor ninth
   c. augmented eleventh
   d. thirteenth
   e. added sixth

   f. quintal
   g. cluster
   h. ninth
   i. eleventh
   j. augmented-major seventh

6. Tap the beat and intone the rhythm of the illustrations from "Other Meters." (pages 182, 183).

7. Add meter signatures to each of the following examples of asymmetrical meter. Tap the beat and intone the rhythm.

a.

b.

c.

8. Add meter signatures to this example of mixed meters.

Now above the staff add an indication that the beat *division* is to remain constant.

PIANO EXERCISES

1. Play and listen to all the scales presented in this chapter.

2. Play and listen to all the chords presented in this chapter.

3. From "Other Meters" (pages 181, 182) play "Oh, How Lovely Is the Evening" in both $\frac{3}{4}$ and $\frac{5}{4}$ meters.

15

Form and Texture

The organization of music into phrases, and phrases into periods, was discussed in Chapter 11. Phrases were found to be unified by events within, such as motivic repetition and sequence, and intervallic and rhythmic structure. This is form *in* music.

Phrases are linked, however, into ever-larger structures that become the forms *of* music. The two forms that long ago became the prototypes of larger musical structures are **binary** and **ternary**.

BINARY FORM   Music in **binary form** is in two parts, A and B. Two unifying characteristics of binary form are:

1. The two parts are linked tonally, as A begins on the tonic and usually ends in the key of the dominant, and B begins in the dominant key and ends on the tonic.

2. Both parts are based on similar musical material, making the form continuous; B then becomes a satisfying and logical completion of A.

The following example illustrates both of these characteristics.

TERNARY FORM

As its name implies, a **ternary form** is in three parts or sections: ABA. The sections are complete within themselves. The most predominant characteristic of ternary form is that of contrast, as the B section may differ in musical material, tonality, style, or texture from the A section. The form is unified by a return of the material of the A section.

"Skye Boat Song" is an example of ternary form. The A sections are in G major. In the B section, contrast is evident in the melodic contour of the phrases and the change in tonality to the relative minor.

Car - ry the lad   that's born to be king   O - ver the sea   to   Skye.

B

Loud the winds howl,   loud the waves roar,   Thun- der clouds rend the   air;

Baf - fled, our foes   stand on the shore,   Fol - low they will   not   dare.

A

Speed, bon-nie boat, like a   bird on the wing,   "On - ward," the sail - ors   cry;

Car - ry the lad   that's born to be king   o - ver the sea   to   Skye.

"Skye Boat Song," copyright J. B. Cramer and Co., Ltd., 99 St. Martin's Lane, London WC2. Used by permission.

RONDO FORM

Rondo form is an extension of ternary form. It is based on the principle of statement, contrast, restatement, and so on. The melodic outline of a five-part rondo—ABACA—is given below.

In addition to the repeat sign, this rondo illustrates *first and second endings* and **da capo al fine**. To play first and second endings (indicated by brackets and the numbers 1 and 2), play through the first ending, return to the beginning, and, omitting the first ending, play through the second ending. *Da capo al fine* (or *D.C. al fine*) is an indication to return to the beginning (*da capo*) and play to the finish (*fine*). The *da capo al fine* provides the final A section for the above rondo.

VARIATION FORM

Variation is a compositional tool or device. For example, music may be changed with such minimal modification as the addition of a passing or neighbor tone or a color tone to a chord; it may also be varied rhythmically. Variation as a form, specifically **theme and variations**, refers to a statement of a theme (that is, a melody) followed by restatements, each different. A theme and variations may be sectional, the theme and each variation ending with a terminal cadence, or continuous, each variation evolving from the one before.

Next is a portion of a theme followed by portions of five (out of a total of eleven) variations by Mozart. Each variation is discussed briefly.

Theme

Mozart, "Ah, vous dirai-je, Maman?"[1]

Variation 1

The rhythm is varied and activity increased by subdivision of the beat and ornamentation of the melody notes.

Variation 3

The quarter-note rhythm of the melody is replaced by **arpeggio** and scale passages in triplet rhythm. The accompaniment is enriched slightly by additional notes.

---

1. *This is the melody we know as "Twinkle, Twinkle, Little Star."*

Variation 5

The rhythm of the melody is changed by dividing the second beat. Rhythmic activity is shared equally by melody and accompaniment.

Variation 6

The melody is intact as the upper notes of right-hand chords. The accompaniment is changed to **trill** and scale passages in beat subdivision.

Variation 8

This variation is in the parallel minor key. The melody becomes a portion of a scale and is imitated or restated at a lower pitch level.

Variation 11

The tempo marking is slow. The rhythm of the melody is syncopated and the beginning of the melody is imitated three times at lower pitch levels.

TEXTURE

Texture refers to the relationship of melody to other components of a tonal environment such as secondary melodies or supporting harmonies.

If melody is alone the texture is **monophonic**.

Are you sleep - ing, are you sleep - ing, Broth - er John, Broth - er John?

If melody is accompanied by chords the texture is **homophonic**. In the first example below, the left-hand accompaniment is rhythmically almost identical to the right-hand melody and consists of broken chords. The second example is a four-part arrangement, the parts rhythmically similar to the melody, which is the top of the right-hand chords.

If melodies combine, the texture is **polyphonic** or **contrapuntal**. The result of this simultaneous sounding of two or more melodies is **counterpoint**.

Counterpoint may be **imitative**, where the melody is restated by another part or voice at a distance of one or several measures. This type of counterpoint is known as **canon** or **round**. In the example below, imitation at the octave begins in the third measure.

Counterpoint may also be nonimitative, where two or more different melodies combine. Below, the nonimitative part, or free counterpoint, is in the bass, and differs melodically and rhythmically from the part above.

CHAPTER EXERCISES

1. Identify each of the following as an example of binary, ternary, rondo, or variation form.

Bach, Bourrée

2. Identify the texture of each of the following examples as monophonic, homophonic, or contrapuntal.

PIANO EXERCISE

1. Perform the melody of Exercise 1(d) of the Chapter Exercises. With the left hand improvise an accompaniment.

Syllables for Rhythmic Reading

Recite numbers to articulated beats, sounding the number for the full value of the note in both simple and compound meters.

- *simple meter*

$\begin{array}{cc}\frac{2}{4} & \end{array}$

    1   2 | 1
  one two   one ——

- *compound meter*

$\frac{6}{8}$

    1   2 | 1
  one two   one ——

When the beat is divided, use the syllable *te* for the division in simple meter and the syllables *lah* and *lee* for the divisions in compound meter.

- *simple meter*

$\frac{2}{4}$

  1 te 2 te | 1
 one te two te one——

- *compound meter*

$\frac{6}{8}$

  1 lah lee 2 lah lee | 1
 one lah lee two lah lee one——

When the beat is subdivided, use the syllable *ta* in both simple and compound meters.

- *simple meter*

- *compound meter*

Examples for practice:

1. simple meter

a.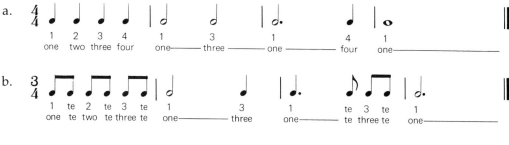

b.

c.

d.

2. compound meter

a.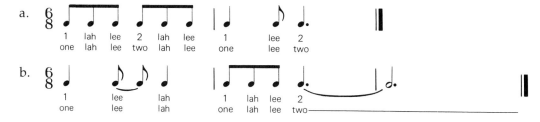

b.

3. triplet

4. duplet

Syllables for Pitch Reading

Fixed *Do* System

The syllable *do* is always C. Every pitch in the chromatic scale has its own syllable.

do   di   re   ri   mi   fa   fi   sol   si   la   li   ti   do

do   ti   te   la   le   sol   se   fa   mi   me   re   ra   do

Movable *Do* System

For any major scale, the tonic is *do*. Each scale step has its corresponding syllable.

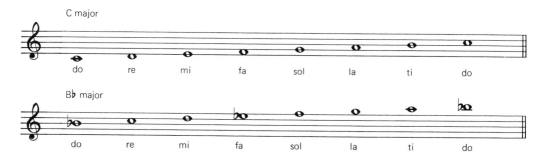

C major

do   re   mi   fa   sol   la   ti   do

B♭ major

do   re   mi   fa   sol   la   ti   do

D major

do — re — mi — fa — sol — la — ti — do

For any minor scale, the tonic is *la* (sixth step of the relative major). Each scale step has its corresponding syllable.

A natural minor

la — ti — do — re — mi — fa — sol — la

Syllables for chromatic alterations are the same as the corresponding syllables of the chromatic scale.

A harmonic minor

la — ti — do — re — mi — fa — si — la

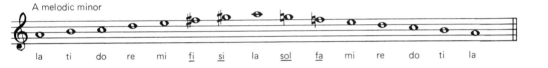

A melodic minor

la — ti — do — re — mi — fi — si — la — sol — fa — mi — re — do — ti — la

Piano Fingering

Finger Numbers

Each finger is identified by number.

left hand (LH)   right hand (RH)

Chords: I, IV, and V7 in Major Keys; i, iv, and V7 in Minor Keys

The hands are in "five-finger" position for tonic chords, with the fifth and first fingers of the left hand on tonic and dominant, and the first and fifth fingers of the right hand on tonic and dominant. For chords requiring movement away from five-finger position, as for IV, iv, and V7, the fingers closest to the notes are used.

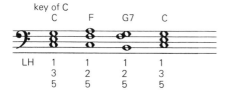

key of E minor
Em Am B7 Em

LH
1 1 1 1
3 2 2 3
5 5 5 5

key of C minor
Cm Fm G7 Cm

RH
5 5 5 5
3 3 4 3
1 1 1 1

Melodies

Begin in five-finger position, if possible, in all keys.

"Lightly Row"

To extend beyond five-finger position, spread the hand between the thumb and the second finger.

"Twinkle, Twinkle, Little Star"

Sometimes the left hand can assist the right hand in playing the melody. Below, the left thumb plays the melody note G below the staff, and then moves *over* the right hand to play the A for "Pop!" The right hand remains in five-finger position.

"Pop! Goes the Weasel"

Often the hand pivots over the thumb in order to assume another five-finger position.

Sometimes a fingering change is made while a note is being sustained, facilitating a shift in hand position.

"Lotus Garden"

Some general principles that apply to the playing of melodies are:

1. As many notes of a melody as possible are played in one hand position.

2. The thumb avoids black keys unless the hand is in a five-finger position beginning on a black key.

3. Often there are choices of fingering for a melody.

4. Fingering must be planned in advance of playing, as adjustments in hand position must constantly be made.

Glossary/Index

a cappella Vocal chorus without instrumental accompaniment.

accelerando Gradually accelerating; written *accel.*

accent Sudden stress; written >. 31

accidental Any chromatic sign not found in the key signature. 69

accompaniment Any part or parts serving as background for voices or instruments carrying the principal part in a composition. 159

acoustics Science of sound. 85

Adagio Slow, leisurely. 34

added tones Tones added to nondominant chords. 181

agogic accent Durational emphasis. 55

air Tune, melody.

alla breve Cut time; written ¢. 42

Allegro Lively, brisk, quick, rapid. 34

alto The deeper of the two main types of women's voices, the other being soprano.

alto clef C clef on the third line of the staff. 25

anacrusis See **upbeat**. 43

Andante "Going"; moderate walking speed. 34

arpeggio Tones of a chord sounding in rapid succession. 192

assai Very; for example, *allegro assai*, very fast. 52

asymmetrical meter Meter that combines beats into groups of two and three. 181

a tempo At the original speed.

augmented interval Interval one half step larger than perfect or major. 96

augmented triad Three-note chord with the intervallic structure major third and augmented fifth above the root. 155

baritone Male voice between bass and tenor.

bar line Vertical line dividing measures on the staff. 32

bass Lowest male voice.

bass clef F clef. 23

beam Line in lieu of flags connecting adjacent notes. 9

beat The pulse plus the time span between one pulse and the next. 31

binary form Organization of music into two sections, AB. 188

blues scale A scale such as the major with "blue" notes added. 178

brace Written {, it connects two or more staves and signifies that the parts on the staves are to be played simultaneously. 25

cadence Close or ending of a phrase, section, or movement. 162

cadence pitch Final melodic pitch of a phrase. 143

canon Contrapuntal music in which a melody is imitated by one or more parts in succession so that all overlap. 195

cantabile In a vocal or singing style.

C clef Movable clef that establishes the location of middle C on the staff. 25

chamber music Vocal or instrumental music suitable for performance in a small room or hall.

chord Three or more tones sounding simultaneously. 154

chord symbol Indication of chord root and chord quality. 158

chord tones Pitches that are part of the harmony. 160

chorus Company of singers; music written for a company of singers, often in four parts; refrain of a song.

chromatic alteration Raising or lowering a pitch by using an accidental.

chromatic half step Half-step interval between two notes with the same letter name. 98

chromatic scale Scale that includes twelve half steps within the octave. 72

chromatic signs Sharp (♯), flat (♭), natural (♮), double sharp (×), and double flat (♭♭). 69, 70

circle of fifths Arrangement of keys in a series of perfect fifths so that the thirteenth key in the series is the same as the first. 82

clef Sign written at the beginning of a staff to fix the position of one pitch. 20

cluster chord Chord built in intervals of a second. 180

coda "Tail"; concluding portion of a movement or composition.

common time $\frac{4}{4}$ meter. 42

compound interval Interval wider than an octave. 98

compound meter Meter in which the beat divides into three equal parts. 104

contrapuntal See **counterpoint.**

counterpoint Musical texture with two or more melodies sounding simultaneously. 195

crescendo Gradually increasing in loudness; written *cresc.* 4

cut time See **alla breve.** 42

da capo al fine Repeat from the beginning to the word

fine; written *D.C. al fine.* 191

dal segno al fine Repeat from the sign ·$· to the word *fine*; written *D.S. al fine.*

decrescendo Gradually diminishing in loudness; written *decresc.* 4

diatonic half step Two tones a half step apart with different letter names. 98

diminished interval Interval one half step smaller than perfect or minor. 96

diminished triad Three-note chord with the intervallic structure minor third and diminished fifth above the root. 155

diminuendo Diminishing in loudness; written *dim.* 4

dolce Sweet, soft.

dominant Fifth degree of a scale. 84

dominant seventh Major-minor seventh chord; written V7. 158

dot A dot placed after a note prolongs its time value by half; a second dot prolongs the time value of the dot preceding it by half. A dot placed over or under a note indicates **staccato.** 12

double bar line Vertical lines (▤) indicating the end of a section or composition. 32

double flat The sign ♭♭, which lowers the pitch of a note two half steps. 70

double period Two consecutive periods. 144

double sharp The sign ×, which raises the pitch of a note two half steps. 70

downbeat Downward conducting stroke indicating the first beat of the measure and the primary accent of the meter. 36

duple meter Metric pattern consisting of two beats. 32

duplet Two-note group re-

sulting from irregular division of a compound beat. 112

duration Length of time a tone persists. 5

dynamic markings See **dynamics.** 5

dynamics Terms and symbols that refer to intensity. 5

eleventh chord Seventh chord with an eleventh added above the root. 180

encore A recall on stage; music repeated after or added to a performance.

enharmonic Different notation of the same pitch, such as C♯ and D♭. 70

F clef Bass clef. 23

fermata Hold (⌢). 91

fine End. 191

first inversion Chord position in which the third of the chord is the lowest note. 156

flat The sign ♭, which lowers the pitch of a note by a half step. 69

form Organization of music. 140, 188

forte Loud, strong; written *f.* 4

fortissimo Very loud; written *ff.* 4

fundamental First partial in the harmonic series. 85

G clef Treble clef. 20

grand staff The two staves, treble and bass, joined by a bracket; also called the great staff. 25

half step Smallest notated interval in Western music. 68

harmonic Pertaining to chords and to the theory and practice of harmony. 6

harmonic cadence Chord pattern at the end of a piece. 162

harmonic interval Tones of an interval sounding simultaneously and represented vertically on the staff. 93

harmonic minor scale Minor scale with a raised seventh step. 130

harmonic series Succession of pitches sounding in sympathy with, and including, a fundamental pitch. 85

harmony Musical combination of tones or chords; a chord; vertical structure of music. 154

hemiola Type of syncopation resulting in a temporary shift in meter from simple to compound or vice versa. 115

hexatonic scale Six-tone scale. 176

homophonic Musical texture consisting of melody accompanied by chords. 194

imitative counterpoint Imitation of a melody or motive in another voice or part.

intensity Degree of loudness of a tone. 4

interval Difference in pitch between two tones. 93

inversion In a simple interval, when the lower note is set an octave higher or the higher note an octave lower; chord in which the lowest tone is not the root. 98

key Tonality of a composition. 80

keynote Tonic; first tone or degree of a scale or key. 79

key signature Sharps or flats written on a staff in a specific order after the clef sign. 80

Larghetto Slow, but not as slow as Largo.

Largo Slowest tempo marking. 34

leading tone Seventh degree

of a scale, a half step from the tonic. 84

ledger line Short line used for writing notes above or below the staff (often written *leger line*). 19

legato "Bound together"; performance of successive pitches in a smooth and connected manner. Indicated by a slur in instrumental music.

Lento Slow (between Andante and Largo). 34

maestoso Broad and majestic.

major interval Qualitative term applied to intervals of a second, third, sixth, and seventh. 96

major scale Series of seven tones in a specific pattern of whole and half steps. 78

major triad Three-note chord with the intervallic structure major third and perfect fifth above the root. 155

measure Metric unit encompassing all the notes and rests between two bar lines.

mediant Third degree of a scale. 84

melodic interval Tones of an interval sounding separately and written one after the other on the staff. 93

melodic minor scale Minor scale with raised sixth and seventh steps ascending and reverting to natural minor descending. 130

melody Succession of individual pitches rhythmically impelled. 140

Meno mosso Less rapid.

meter Grouping of beat patterns. 32

meter signature Two numbers written in vertical alignment denoting meter. 32

metronome Apparatus that sounds beats, named Mael-

zel's metronome for its reputed inventor. 35

mezzo "Half"; *mezzo forte* (*mf*), softer than *f*, *mezzo piano* (*mp*), louder than *p*. 4

middle C The pitch C nearest the center of the piano keyboard. 21

minor interval Interval one half step smaller than major. 96

minor scale Series of seven tones in a specific pattern of whole and half steps. 126

minor triad Three-note chord with the intervallic structure minor third and perfect fifth above the root. 155

mixed meter Dissimilar metric patterns occurring in close proximity. 182

M.M. Maelzel's metronome. 35

Moderato At a moderate speed. 34

modes Diatonic seven-tone scales other than major and minor. 174

modulate To pass from one key to another.

molto Very; for example, Molto adagio, very slow.

monophonic Musical texture of melody alone. 194

morendo Dying away.

motive Short melodic-rhythmic figure. 142

natural The sign ♮, which cancels a sharp, flat, double sharp, or double flat. 69

natural minor scale See **minor scale.**

neighbor tone Nonchord tone connecting by step two chord tones of the same pitch. 162

ninth chord Seventh chord with a ninth added above the root. 180

nonchord tone A pitch not part of the harmony. 160

nonharmonic tone See **nonchord tone.**

nontertian chord Chord built in intervals other than thirds. 180

notation Representation of sound on paper. 1

note Musical symbol for a sound. 8

octave Eighth tone of a diatonic scale; duplication of a letter name. 26

octave sign An 8 followed by a dotted line signifying an octave higher if written above the staff, an octave lower if written below the staff. 26

opera Form of drama with music, soloists, chorus, orchestra, and staging.

opus Work, abbreviated op.; an opus number is the chronological identification of the work of a composer.

overtone A partial above the fundamental in the harmonic series.

parallel keys Major and minor keys that share the same tonic. 129

partials Tones of the harmonic series. 6, 85

passing tone Nonchord tone connecting by step two different chord tones. 162

pentatonic scale Five-tone scale with two intervals of a third. 177

perfect interval Qualitative term applied to the prime, fourth, fifth, and octave. 96

period Complete musical thought, often consisting of two or three phrases and ending with a terminal cadence. 144

phrase One section of a period; musical passage complete in itself. 143

pianissimo Very soft; written *pp*. 4

piano Soft; written *p*. 4

pitch Position of a tone in a high-low sound spectrum. 2

poco Little; for example, Poco adagio, somewhat slow.

poco a poco Little by little.

polyphonic Musical texture with two or more melodies sounding simultaneously. 195

Prestissimo Very fast. 114

Presto Fast, rapid (faster than Allegro). 34

primary chord Tonic, subdominant, or dominant; that is, one of three fundamental chords of a key. 156

prime Two tones on the same line or space. 93

progressive cadence Cadence ending on a chord other than the tonic, usually the dominant. 162

quadruple meter Metric pattern consisting of four beats. 32

quartal chord Chord built in intervals of a fourth. 180

quintal chord Chord built in intervals of a fifth. 180

rallentando Gradually slower; written *rall*.

relative keys Major and minor keys that share the same key signature. 132

repeat The sign ≣ or signs ≣ ≣. 125

rest Measured silence. 13

rhythm Effect produced by varied durations of tones and rests. 36

ritardando Gradually slower; written *rit*.

rondo Music organized into sections, one section alternating with contrasting sections. 190

root The tone that gives a chord its name. 154

root position Vertical arrangement of chord tones in which the root is the lowest pitch. 155

round See **canon**.

scale Arrangement of pitches in successive order. 72

score Systematic arrangement of vocal or instrumental parts of a composition on separate staves one above the other.

secondary chord Supertonic, mediant, submediant, or leading-tone chord. 156

second inversion Chord position in which the fifth of the chord is the lowest note. 156

sequence Repetition of a musical idea at a different pitch level. 143

seventh chord Four-note chord consisting of a triad and a seventh added above the root. 157

sharp The sign ♯, which raises the pitch of a note a half step. 69

simple meter Meter in which the beat divides into multiples of two. 35

slur Curved line used to extend a syllable over two or more notes of different pitch; in instrumental music, used to indicate that successive pitches are to be performed smoothly. 102

soprano Highest female voice.

staccato "Disconnected"; performance of a note or succession of notes in a detached manner; indicated by a dot over or under each note.

staff Five parallel lines and four intervening spaces on which music is notated. 14, 19

subdominant Fourth degree of a scale. 84

submediant Sixth degree of a scale. 84

subtonic Whole step below the tonic, as in the natural minor scale. 130

supertonic Second degree of a scale. 84

syncopation Irregular rhythmic accentuation. 55

tempo Rate of speed at which beats recur. 34

tempo markings Terms indicating the relative speed of the beat. 34

tenor Highest male voice.

tenor clef C clef on the fourth line of the staff. 25

terminal cadence Cadence with the tonic as the concluding chord. 162

ternary form Organization of music into three sections, ABA. 189

tertian chord Chord built in intervals of a third. 180

tessitura In a piece of music, the general "lie" or compass of a voice or instrument in relation to its entire pitch range. 25

tetrachord Four-note scale pattern. 79

texture Relationship of the melodic and harmonic components of a musical composition. 194

theme and variations Organization of music into a statement of a theme followed by restatements, each different. 191

thirteenth chord Seventh chord with a thirteenth added above the root. 180

tie Curved line connecting two adjacent notes of the same pitch, indicating they are to be sounded as one tone and held for their combined time value. 12

timbre Tone quality. 6

tonality Key in which a composition is written; relationship of the other tones to the tonic. 80

tone Sound that is the result of regular vibration. 1

tonic First note or keynote of a scale. 79, 84

transpose Perform or write the same piece in a different key. 86

treble clef G clef. 20

triad Three-tone chord consisting of root, third, and fifth in ascending order. 154

trill Rapid alternation of two adjacent notes. 193

triple meter Metric pattern consisting of three beats. 32

triplet Group of three equal notes sounded in the time of two of like value. 54

troppo Too, too much; for example, Non troppo adagio, not too slow.

unison A tone of the same pitch as a given tone; in ensemble music, a lower or higher octave sounding with the original tone.

upbeat One or more unaccented notes before the primary accent at the beginning of a measure. 36, 43

variation form See **theme and variations**.

whole step Difference in pitch equal to two half steps. 68

whole-tone scale Six-tone scale consisting of a series of six whole steps. 176